Woolwich 18: October

e Afternoon at Longreach Mustering
ndermention'd have sent your Honour
On this Occasion take leave to _
ichols the Lieutenant inform'd me,
was on Thursday in the Afternoon
ing Captains with Fortyone _
ll put on board the Thunder that
he was signing a Receipt for the
Tender some of the Prest Men gather
nner, forced out of the

LIVING
THE
PAST

ENGLISH HERITAGE

LIVING THE PAST

VAL HORSLER

941

PHOTOGRAPHY BY
DERRY BRABBS

WEIDENFELD & NICOLSON

First published in the United Kingdom in 2003
by Weidenfeld & Nicolson, in association
with English Heritage.

Distributed in the United States of America by
Sterling Publishing Co., Inc.
387 Park Avenue South
New York
NY 10016-8810

A CIP catalogue record for this book is available from
the British Library.
ISBN 0297 84312 5

Editor Catherine Bradley

Designer Nigel Soper
Indexer Drusilla Calvert

Typeset in Garamond & Frutiger
Printed and bound in Italy by Printer Trento S.r.l.

Weidenfeld & Nicolson
The Orion Publishing Group
Wellington House
125 Strand
London WC2R 0BB

PRECEDING PAGES
MAIN PICTURE: Eat, drink and be merry: authentic food, drink and costume – including a magnificent periwig – recreate the Stuart era in a picnic at Kirby Hall, Northamptonshire.

TITLE PAGE: An aristocratic Georgian lady shields her face from the sun at a re-enactment of one of George II's visits to Marble Hill House, Surrey.

OPPOSITE: The burning of a reconstructed Viking longboat, performed by re-enactment groups such as Regia Anglorum, powerfully evokes a remote but fascinating past.

PAGES 6–7:
(TOP ROW, LEFT TO RIGHT): West Stow Anglo-Saxon Village, Suffolk; the Legio XX Valeria Victrix on Hadrian's Wall, Northumberland; scones made from a Tudor recipe at Kirby Hall, Northamptonshire; absorbing news from the 1930s at Eltham Palace, southeast London; authentic embroidery at the Norman Festival, Castle Acre Priory, Norfolk; Stuart musical instruments, entertaining King Charles II on a progress to Audley End House, Essex.

(BOTTOM ROW, LEFT TO RIGHT): an ARP warden at the Blitz Experience, Imperial War Museum, London; a Viking warrior, Tynemouth Priory, Northumberland; baking bread in a traditional oven at West Stow Anglo-Saxon Village, Suffolk; George II and a courtier at Marble Hill House, Surrey; jousting at the Norman Festival, Castle Acre Priory, Norfolk; Tudor cooking at Kirby Hall, Northamptonshire.

'There is a dream that all re-enactors have. That somewhere there is
… a place where they can get up in the morning and look out of …
a real house at an undisturbed and idealized landscape where there
is nothing out of place … nothing that imposes upon the quiet but
deeply felt urge to think "it must have been just like this". … There
will be times when the axe handle is so cold with frost that it is
difficult to chop the wood; times when the fire won't draw; times
when the porridge sets; times when the children sniffle and miss the
telly. However, there will be occasions when the thunder crashes
across the sky and the wolves howl at the lightning, and it comes to
you just why our ancestors were pagans.'

KIM SIDDORN, REGIA ANGLORUM

CONTENTS

FOREWORD BY DR DAVID STARKEY — 8

INTRODUCTION — 10

1 HOW TO EXPERIENCE THE PAST — 14

2 THE ROMANS IN BRITAIN — 38

3 SAXONS, VIKINGS AND NORMANS — 62

4 MEDIEVAL LIFE — 84

5 Tudors, Stuarts and the Civil War   104

6 Life in Georgian Times   126

7 The Victorian Age   148

8 The Early 20th Century   170

Useful Names and Addresses   186

Further Reading   188

Index   189

Acknowledgements   192

Foreword

I N MY INTRODUCTION TO *The Reign of Henry VIII* I wrote that 'to transfer from Tudor Whitehall to the modern White House requires little more than a change of clothes'. In a sense this book shows the reverse to be equally true. English Heritage produces the biggest programme of historical re-enactment in the world, some 400 events encompassing over a thousand years of history and hundreds of different activities from fighting 18th-century battles or jousting in medieval tournaments to making Iron Age shelters. To take part the re-enactors don authentic dress of traditional fabrics made in time-honoured ways, wield weapons forged as they would have been and eat period meals from wooden or pewter platters. They immerse themselves in every detail of their chosen past.

These new historians don't want just to read about history or watch it on television but also to experience what it was really like to live in different historical eras. To leave the long hours and sober suits of the money markets to ride into battle without stirrups, or the uniform of the supermarket checkout to don the dazzling clothes of an Elizabethan courtier, is to make history come alive.

This book is crammed with illustrations of people doing just that, startling photographs in full colour of the Ermine Street Guard training, or a young soldier donning his full battle kit, or 19th-century mechanics tinkering with their creation – the world's first steam locomotive. But it is not just about people in authentic clothes going about their allotted tasks; it is also about the locations where actual events occurred, where the footprints of history are ineradicably marked on battlefield or castle, or medieval hall.

For academic historians the task is to throw new light on the great march of events, to evalute and re-evaluate the politics, the affairs of state, the intrigues and shifting alliances that make up 'history' as a discipline. There are the concrete facts: the great events, the dynasties, the disasters, the triumphs – the rich tapestry of recorded history stretching back in Britain to the Romans and beyond, when chroniclers first set down for succeeding generations what was happening in their world; but there are also eons of time where conjecture and archaeology are all we have to go on. For non-academic historians, the fascination is often to recapture the detail of past lives. It is the graffiti on the wall of a prison or the sonnet scratched into the glass of a casement window that quickens the pulse.

It is this aspect of history that television programmes or a book such as *Living the Past* excel in; the sights, sounds and smells of the past come alive for the viewer and reader. Although it is true to say that the re-enactor can never fully relive the past, any more than the academic historian can fully understand it or penetrate its mental world, we nonetheless gain a greater understanding of life in different eras of our history, in authentic as well as entertaining detail.

DR DAVID STARKEY

Introduction

THE PAST IS EVERYWHERE AROUND US, even in our modern, hi-tech world. History and archaeology on television are as popular as the ubiquitous cookery, gardening and home makeover programmes, and academic historians have become celebrity presenters. Yet it is arguable that today's population is more divorced from its past than at any previous time in history. The 20th century, preceded by the Victorian genius for innovation, saw more change and development in a short time span than ever before, severing us decisively from our ancestors, whose way of life we can now barely comprehend. Those living 100 years ago would probably relate more closely to the people of the 18th century than to ourselves. Is it perhaps in this alienation that our fascination lies?

For fascinated we are. Time travel is an enduring fantasy. Genealogy is one of the most common uses for the internet, and the website of the Public Record Office (now the National Archives) famously crashed under the volume of hits on the newly available 1901 census. The physical legacy of the past also exerts a powerful spell. More people visit historic properties than go to football matches. The organizers of the Queen Mother's lying-in-state and funeral in 2002 were taken aback by the numbers of people who queued and lined the streets – people of all ages and from all walks of life, many of them attracted by the chance to participate in a historic event. From national pageantry to local traditions such as well-dressing and cheese-rolling, and from choosing to watch history on television to discovering who lived in our houses 100 years ago, we seek to be connected to a past that is both grand and individual, both national and local.

It is a truism for those who seek to justify – and explain – this desire that we must understand the past in order to understand the present. Indeed we must! We are part of a continuum and our roots are an important binding force. But for most of us, the stimulus lies in something simpler – an urge to find out what it was really like to live 100 – or 1000 – years ago. The history that used to be taught in schools – full of dates

and lists – is no longer adequate; we want to know what life was actually like, how the ordinary people of past centuries lived and died. We relish the process of discovery.

'Living history' responds to exactly this interest and the questions it poses. What can it have been like to have to grow or catch your food before you could eat it? And how did you eat it before the fork was invented? How were clothes fastened before there were buttons? When a poor man possessed only a single garment that was worn night and day, what did he and it smell like? Living history allows us to be detectives – to explore the minutiae of the everyday past through living museums, re-enactments, places and documents that bring the past alive and bring us closer to people who were once as real as ourselves.

Our basic problem, of course, is that it is impossible, with 21st-century eyes and brains, completely to experience the past. We may think we know a historic site well, and may feel that we have learned a great deal about its inhabitants, but the world of the people who patrolled those battlements or looked out of that window is beyond contemporary imagination. What can it have been like to have to walk under Micklegate Bar in York early in 1461, with the decomposing heads of the Duke of York and his son, Edmund, Earl of Rutland, louring down at you? Would you have been part of the crowd at the public burning of Hugh Latimer and Nicholas Ridley in Broad Street, Oxford, nearly 100 years later in October 1555? In your own smaller world, too, how would you have endured the death of yet another of your babies, born in pain and hope? How would you have survived the terrible 'not knowing', when the one and only son you'd managed to raise to adulthood had been called up into the lord's levies for someone else's distant war? It is hard today to imagine the terror of childbirth in centuries before modern drugs and medical knowledge – or any reliable means of preventing pregnancy.

ABOVE: Living history interpreters are not only dedicated researchers into the minutiae of dress and accoutrements, but are also often skilled in the arts and crafts of their period. Here a quartet plays chamber music in the authentically Georgian setting of the Pantiles in Tunbridge Wells. The players use period instruments and follow 18th-century performance techniques. For example, the cellist does not use a spike but holds the cello between his knees.

ABOVE: Troops from the 47th Regiment of Foot parade at Lyddington Bede House, part of a recreated recruitment for King George during the American War of Independence. Meticulously observed details of uniforms and weaponry include diagonal crossbelts for cartridge cases and backpacks, anchored with a tight chest strap that caused breathing difficulties for many soldiers. Authenticity has other problems, too: the material used for the famous 18th-century redcoats, although warm, is impossibly heavy when wet and takes ages to dry out.

How did families cope with the strong possibility that they would lose a wife and mother in childbirth? Would the pains of everyday life, from toothache to arthritis, have been lessened by the certain knowledge that you could do nothing about them?

The huge technological strides forward of the last century dug a deeper chasm between us and our forebears than ever before. In the West, we now live in homes in which central heating, electric light and running water are standard; refrigeration allows us to buy food from all over the world, in and out of season, and to store it in our own fridges and freezers at home; electricity means that we no longer have to rise with the dawn and go to bed in the dark; entertainment is there at the flick of a switch or the push of a remote control button. Yet only 50 years ago I grew up in a house without central heating, a telephone, a television, or a fridge; my grandparents' house still had an outside, non-flushing lavatory until the 1960s. Today's necessities were luxuries then – the gulf is enormous.

And we sense, imperceptibly, the loss of an anchor. Is it because we have moved so far away from our past that our obsession with history is growing apace? At a time of radical change in the way we live, work and enjoy ourselves, we are in danger of isolation within the continuum of human life; we feel disconnected. So we increasingly look back at the past and try to understand and relate to it.

This book is about realizing that desire. It looks at the various ways of experiencing the past – evocative sites, living museums, re-enactment events, documents – and uses them to show how our understanding can develop. We can never really know 'what it was like'; but living history helps to provide valuable glimpses of a vanished – but always intriguing and compelling – world.

We all have roots in the past. Our families extend back into it; houses, streets and towns were shaped by it; and it made possible all aspects of our daily lives. Yet those who inhabited it often elude our understanding. Living history brings them closer to us by

How to EXPERIENCE the PAST

recreating the practical details of their lives – what they wore, ate and lived in; how they fought, farmed or worked in new industrial towns. Events cover all periods, from prehistory to the 1940s; they are often held in historic locations or at living history museums that bring a region's past to life. Documents are also part of living history, linking us to the people who produced them and the events they describe.

1

Looking into the past

'The past is a foreign country: they do things differently there.'

L P HARTLEY, *THE GO-BETWEEN*

CONSCIOUSLY OR NOT, WE ALL HAVE A VIVID SENSE OF HISTORY – often based on clichés and misconceptions, but nonetheless powerful. This vision may be tinged with horror or a sentimental nostalgia: gap-toothed hags with matted hair leering in the smoky shadows of a narrow London street; or rural idylls, where lusty youths and blushing maidens gambolled in endless golden sunshine. Both distort reality, and the more we can find out about what life in the past was really like, the closer we can come to those who inhabited it.

We need to recognize, first and foremost, that there are not only many similarities between us and our predecessors, but also real, fundamental differences. Reason tells us that, in all probability, the people of the past were very much like us – they loved and cared for their children and mourned when they died; they enjoyed festivals and celebrations and lying around doing nothing on days of rest; they were sickened by injustice and cruelties. But in many ways they are still tantalizingly alien: we would be unlikely to understand their speech; their food would be unpalatable; they would die of illnesses that can now be treated with modern medicine and a day or so in bed. Most of all, their lives were limited by lack of education, lack of transport and the rigid social and class structures.

Their assumptions and perspectives – their whole experience of life – were consequently and genuinely very different from our own.

RIGHT: Although they cannot aspire to the same scale of magnificence, recreations of royal progresses are memorable events. Here, Tudor entertainers and courtiers at Kenilworth Castle sing rounds and madrigals to please Elizabeth – on the site she visited 500 years ago.

ABOVE: This elaborately carved effigy in the north transept at Winchester Cathedral shows the importance of such monuments to people in the past. In centuries when death and religious observance were at the heart of everyday life, tombs expressed social status as well as hope for the afterlife.

ABOVE: A magnificent heavy horse at Ryedale Folk Museum prepares to pull a hay wagon in the recreation of a 1940s harvest. Even in the 1950s, it was believed that horses would always be used in upland farming, so recent is the arrival of modern technology.

Lifespans were shorter: the average for a medieval man was 30–35 years, and even in 1840, whereas the rural gentry and the professional classes might expect to see their 50th birthdays, many labourers in the industrial cities would be lucky to see their 20th. The average for women was lower because of the perils of childbirth, and death in infancy was common for all classes, no respecter of rank or wealth. Analysis of bodies buried between 1729 and 1852 in the vaults under Christ Church, Spitalfields, London, showed that over half of them were aged under 21. One of those buried there was an illiterate weaver's wife, who raised nine of her ten children to adulthood, in contrast to a member of a wealthy Huguenot family who lost all six of her children in infancy. Nor did it help to be royal: Queen Anne endured 18 pregnancies, with 13 resulting in still-births; four of her five children who survived birth died in infancy, and the only son who survived infancy died at the age of 11; how heartbreaking that boy's death must have been! It was not until the middle of the 19th century – a mere 150 years ago – that infant mortality began to decline.

Places were different, too. Despite the visible remains of the past – buildings we would recognize if we could travel back in time – the Britain of centuries ago would indeed have seemed a 'foreign country'. The country was emptier, and towns and cities were small. Compared with the 2001 United Kingdom population of over 58.7 million, estimates for the Roman period range from two to four million, declining to around one and a half million at the time of Domesday Book, which began the process of measuring the realm in 1086. Centuries before any effective medical treatment was available, the devastating Black Death of 1348–50 killed about a third of the entire population of England, including nearly half that of London; it took 200 years for population levels to recover. Even in 1700, the population of England was only around six million.

The buildings would also have looked different, and not just because what are now ruins would have been complete and in use. Only 100 years ago many of today's chocolate-box thatched cottages, now the homes of wealthy families, were dilapidated hovels lived in by the rural poor. Photographs 'then and now' are vivid illustrations of how such houses have gone up in the world. Communities were closer. It is a modern cliché that it takes years for urban dwellers moving to the country to be spoken to by their neighbours; but historically in rural areas strangers were curiosities, menacing perhaps,

Order to Lord chiefe Justice to enquire after ye Ryott at the house infected

Upon Information given unto this Board, that the house, the Signe of the ship in the New buildings, in St Giles in the fields, was shutt up as suspected to bee Infected with the Plague, & a Crosse and paper fixed, on the doore; And that the sd Cross & paper were taken off, & the door opened, in a Riotous manner, & the people of the house permitted, to goe abroad into the street promiscuously, with others; It is this day ordered (his Matie present in Councell) that the Lord chiefe Justice, of his Maties Bench, & other his Maties Justices of the peace, for the County of Middlesex, bee and are hereby desired, to make diligent & strict enquiry, after the offendors in the sd Ryott; And inflict vpon them, for such of them as they shall find) the severest punishmt, the Rigor of the Law, will allow, against offendrs in actions, of soe dangerous a Consequence; And soe much to the Contempt of his Maty orders as theis;

unpredictable and frightening. Migration has always been with us: the movements of whole nations have shaped the face of the planet. But today such movements are both broader and more individual than ever before, with people of hundreds of different nationalities living together in cities across the world.

The world of the past was small and local. Most country people in medieval times spent the whole of their lives in their own village, never travelling more than a few miles outside it, reliant for news of the wider world on occasional itinerant traders. Parson Woodforde recalls in his diary how the news of Waterloo took many months to reach his rural parish. Even at the end of the 19th century, it was not unusual for village dwellers to know little outside a very narrow horizon. In contrast, modern perceptions are shaped by television and the familiarity with the world's wildly varied geography and cultures that it brings. Expert camerawork allows us to see into the deepest depths of the oceans, and satellites show us our world from space. News of faraway events arrives immediately: on 11 September 2001, millions of people the world over learned instantly what had happened in the United States, and turned on their televisions to watch as the drama and horror unfolded.

Such instant, global communication is the unique experience of people today. Telecommunications have, within living memory, transformed our lives. In the 1950s, the telephone was a large, black, Bakelite instrument that sat in solitary splendour in the (usually)

ABOVE: Documents from the National Archives show how ordinary people responded to dramatic historical events. In 1665, as the Great Plague ravaged the country, houses thought to be infected were closed by public order, and their inhabitants left to die. This account describes how one group rebelled and broke out of their houses 'in a riotous manner'; it notes that they are to be pursued and punished for their lack of public spiritedness.

OPPOSITE: Military re-enactments cover all aspects of conflict, including medical care, and provide authentic roles for women and boys as well as men. In this recreation of a Peninsular War battle, mounted at Kirby Hall, Northamptonshire, women assist the field surgeon. Wounds from muskets, cannon and sabres made this a particularly bloody conflict, and the death toll was high.

ABOVE: This farmhouse from Llangadfan, Powys, was built in 1678 and re-erected at the Museum of Welsh Life in 1955. A typical timber-framed house of mid-Wales and the Marches, its fireplace is opposite the only doorway and panels between the wall timbers are filled with woven hazel rods daubed with clay. The hall or main living room was originally open to the roof (as was usual in the Middle Ages); a loft was added in 1708.

draughty and unheated hallway of the house; nowadays it is not unusual to have phones in several rooms, complemented by ever-smaller, palm-sized mobiles and computers linked to the internet. Early computers in the 1950s took up whole rooms; now they are carried in briefcases.

Beyond gadgets, however, are the social changes which make it impossible to imagine oneself back in the past in any meaningful way: the inequalities of class then, contrasted with the death of deference now; the paternalistic world-view then, as opposed to the influence of feminism now; education for the few then, and for all (in the world's developed nations) now; the Christian religion as the bedrock of society then, and now just one strand of a multicultural society. Added to these is the factor of security. Despite the horrors of recent world events, most of us in the West expect to live out our allotted spans unthreatened by the immediacy of war, deadly disease or fatal accident. Not for us (cross fingers) the unpredictability of life in the past. The rapid globalization of society has created a cosmopolitan world in which our own history and heritage are only part of life's rich pattern. All of this alienates us further from our ancestors.

Yet the fascination remains – the urge to find out and experience *what it was really like*. So how do we set about it?

Visiting sites

THERE IS WHAT WOULD TODAY BE CALLED A WORKTOP in the medieval kitchens at Haddon Hall in Derbyshire that is marked by a series of holes and craters. This was where food was prepared and dough kneaded every day for the household's bread, wearing the wood away in the process; as one area of the surface eroded to the point of being unusable, the kitchen staff moved on to the next.

This evocative little vignette of life in the past calls up many images. It tells of a time when the daily bread really was just that: prepared and cooked every day, at home, by a household member; no popping round to the shop for a loaf, or taking one out of the freezer! The bread-making activity itself, a regular chore going on for the year after year it would have taken to wear such craters and holes in the wood, hints at the bigger picture: large, extended families and long family histories; decades and centuries of births and deaths; excitements and tedious repetition; the relentless routine of daily life contrasted with special celebrations and festivals.

We visit houses such as Haddon Hall for just this sort of tangible contact with the people of the past, as well as for the magnificence that is perhaps more likely to be found at grander houses such as Blenheim Palace and Audley End House – huge mansions built by kings and nobles. When such buildings first opened to the public,

ABOVE: The East Bedroom in Harewood House, Yorkshire, once used by Edwin Lascelles. The décor is by Robert Adam and all the furniture, including the bed, is by Thomas Chippendale. The 18th century witnessed the building of many houses such as Harewood (1759–71), as wealthy owners displayed their cultivated taste.

RIGHT: Today's visitors want to see all over the grand houses of the past, both upstairs and downstairs. The original kitchen at Brodsworth Hall in Yorkshire contains a fascinating array of pots, pans and kitchen implements, as well as the Butler's Pantry and Still Room – all as they were when the kitchen was abandoned in the 1920s.

RIGHT: An aerial view of Chysauster in Cornwall, showing the remains of Iron Age dwellings surrounded by Celtic field systems. The stone-built houses, with their paved courtyards, form one of the oldest village streets in the country; it is possible to imagine them as quite cosy when roofed, although wintertime would have been a bleak experience.

'I'd probably have been a servant in a great house, not one of the toffs, so I like to see "below stairs" where I might have lived in those days…'

little attention was paid to 'below stairs'; kitchens, servants' quarters and the parts behind the green baize door were rarely regarded as of interest, and survivals such as Haddon Hall's medieval kitchen were rare. But now, increasingly, visitors want to see behind the scenes. At Brodsworth Hall in Yorkshire, a mere stripling of a stately home, built in the 1850s, the grand Victorian kitchen was simply abandoned and locked up in the 1920s when the family decamped to a smaller, more modern kitchen; it is now the *pièce de résistance* of a visit, its boilers and ranges and arrays of utensils tugging us back to an era when even quite modest households were served by armies of domestics.

Brodsworth Hall, like the National Trust's Calke Abbey and Chastleton, illustrates another recent trend in the way these houses are opened to the public. Some of them are now shown to us warts and all, not gussied up to some often fictitious 'golden age' of their history. We no longer want them ossified in time; we want to see how they have grown and developed along the way, the effect that people have had on them.

LEFT AND BELOW:
Neolithic wetland trackways have been reconstructed at the Peat Moors Centre in Somerset, where original examples were discovered in the peat landscape of the Somerset Levels. Living history interpreters at the centre, wearing the authentic wool clothes of the Iron Age, maintain a recreated track; here they are repairing sections of the wood supports that sink into the bog through use.

The homes of the more distant past are even more fascinating, not least because they were the dwellings of 'ordinary people'. The Neolithic village at Skara Brae in Orkney looks quite comfortable with its ancient 'furniture': platform beds, stone dressers for storage and display, central hearths for warmth and food (presumably one's eyes got used to the smoke) and drainage channels in the floor to keep damp at bay, or even to provide a simple lavatory system. Barrows litter the landscape around Stonehenge, and ancient tracks, preserved in peat, cross the Somerset Levels. Prehistoric field boundaries on upland moors, still standing and in use, point to the age-old continuity of agriculture. It really is spine-tingling to walk across a Midlands field of ridge and furrow and realize that you are treading on the practically untouched remains of medieval strip farming.

Other places are charged with history, too. Battlefields where dynasties died and the future was shaped, local parish churches that have witnessed the christenings, marriages and burials of generations, the mills that ground corn for the centuries of daily bread, the shops and worn cobbled alleys of Victorian towns, all have a story to tell. Sites on the tourist itinerary may provide a specific focus, but we are also increasingly aware that history is all around us, and that we can get close to the people of the past just by walking down the street.

Living museums

At Warwick Castle, the 'Kingmaker' exhibition recreates the day before the battle of Barnet in 1471 at which Richard Neville, Earl of Warwick, was killed. The entrance is next to the stables, and as you approach the door, your nose wrinkles, and you think to yourself 'How disgusting! Someone has peed!' And then you realize that it is all part of the authenticity. Stables, then as now, are smelly places.

This is the essence of living museums – the recreation of the past in all its reality. Tools and trinkets, costumes and weapons, furniture and foods are shown, and used, in appropriate settings. History is tangible and dynamic, not enclosed in glass cases, leading us through our senses into a living environment. There are smells of a more remote past, for example, at Jorvik in the city of York where the vile odours of the midden come as an unpleasant shock countered by more appetising food smells. Jorvik is located on the Viking settlement excavated beneath present-day Coppergate, and its reconstructed houses and workshops, complemented by lifelike figures with authentic Viking faces, vividly evoke the bustling street scene.

At other living museums costumed interpreters, both volunteers and professional actors, play out the minutiae of everyday life, mingling with the crowd to give a real flavour of the past. At Blists Hill, part of the Ironbridge range of museums, a historic branch of Lloyds Bank exchanges modern cash for pre-decimal tokens to spend at the butcher's, the sweet shop or the hardware store, all offering the goods available to people of the time.

The doctor's surgery at Blists Hill, with its array of horrific-looking implements as well as pills and potions, is a potent reminder that pain and illness in the past could only rarely be effectively treated.

ABOVE: Bede's World recreates Anglo-Saxon life in northern England around AD 700, when well-kept weapons were an essential part of everyday life. Knives were more common than swords; shields, with their distinctive central iron bosses and wooden leather surrounds, have been excavated from many Anglo-Saxon male graves.

RIGHT: Blists Hill is a recreated Victorian town in the Severn Valley at Ironbridge, cradle of the Industrial Revolution and now a World Heritage Site. Reconstructed buildings, living history interpreters and authentic transport reveal the different faces of life in a thriving industrial town.

Living museums are about the horrible features of the past as well as the pleasant. Some illustrate terrifying situations, such as life in the trenches during World War I or in cities during the Blitz in World War II. Both the Trench and the Blitz Experiences at the Imperial War Museum work through the senses, combining darkness with confused flashes of light, plus the smells and sounds of whizzbangs or air raids.

All over Britain, living museums and open air museums use historic sites, buildings and animals to recreate past environments. Norfolk Rural Life Museum at Gressenhall has a working farm stocked with animals native to the region, including Suffolk Punch horses, as well as an apple orchard, a recreated village street and traditional cottages with their gardens. Ryedale Folk Museum in Yorkshire has craft workshops, as do the Museum of East Anglian Life in Suffolk and Amberley Working Museum in Sussex: the blacksmith, cooper, saddler, wheelwright, walking stick maker and other rural trades are featured. The East Anglian Museum at Stowmarket has rare breeds and their two Suffolk Punch horses, Remus and Byron, can often be found hard at work on the site. All these museums allow visitors to try their hand at traditional crafts, and experience the difficulties of life before modern technology. Many also have working examples of the village shops on which rural communities depended.

The Open Air Museum at Beamish in County Durham recreates life in the north of England in the early 1800s and 1900s, with working farms of both periods, railway trips, a colliery village and a town street complete with shops, bank and a pub. The Black Country Living Museum, Dudley, does the same for the industrial midlands; visitors can go down a coal mine and through canal tunnels, and can also walk through streets and landscapes that bring the past to authentic life. Buildings from across Wales are reconstructed at the Museum of Welsh Life at St Fagan's, Cardiff, showing the daily lives of ordinary people over several centuries. Bede's World, named after the famous 8th-century monk, is recreated at Jarrow where he lived 1300 years ago, with demonstrations of calligraphy and metalwork as well as Anglo-Saxon living history and a working farm of the period.

Some living museums are dedicated specifically to conservation and experimentation. Like Jorvik, West Stow Anglo-Saxon village is built on the site of a real excavated village; its reconstructed buildings and other living experiments explore archaeologists' views about life in the past. Butser Ancient Farm in Hampshire is also a remarkable

ABOVE: The shop at Gressenhall is fitted out and stocked as a general store in the 1930s. The large tins hold tobacco which, like other goods sold loose, was weighed out to the customer's order. The packets contain dried goods like raisins and sennapods, while in the bottles are flavourings such as cochineal and gravy browning. Small items of haberdashery, such as bootlaces, pins and press studs, are kept in the little drawers. From these hang the jug used to measure out liquid goods and the butter pat, which pressed into shape a portion of butter bought from a large block.

place – an 'open-air laboratory' that rigorously tests theories about how people lived in the Iron Age and Roman times. Butser's owners rear the nearest possible equivalents to ancient livestock and grow ancient varieties of crops, using reconstructed equipment that leaves in place the weeds that infested fields in the days before pesticides. They build and furnish Iron Age roundhouses, guessing at and investigating practical methods of construction, and note how they develop and decay. The vital methods of grain storage – essential for survival through winter and spring – are also tested, above and below ground. Serious archaeology it may be; yet their immediacy to everyday life makes Butser's investigations continually fascinating. Discoveries are explained to visitors, students and school groups, bringing them closer to the realities of distant lives.

The difficulty of approaching people from the very remote past is tackled at the Peat Moors Centre in Somerset, which explores prehistoric life in the wetlands of the Somerset Levels. This is also a working archaeological 'laboratory' in which Iron Age houses have been reconstructed, along with the Levels' famous prehistoric wooden trackways. The centre also runs intriguing practical courses on metalwork, pottery-making, spinning and dyeing and the manufacture of wattle and daub, designed for school groups and individuals. Here you can make a bronze mirror or a silver neck torc, walk carefully along a reconstructed Neolithic trackway or get stuck in on a wattle and daub wall; and also join in the festivities on the ancient quarter days, culminating at the end of October with the magnificent burning of a wicker man at Samhain.

BELOW: Hands-on activities at the Peat Moors Centre introduce visitors to skills that would have been essential to their ancestors. Pits on the site contain daub, a mixture of clay, dung and chopped straw (left) used over a wooden wattle framework to make the walls of prehistoric structures (right). The mudlarks involved in wattling and daubing are fun today, but it would have been a demanding, dirty chore when shelter from the weather depended on your efforts.

Stepping into the past

FACTS, DATES, LISTS OF KINGS AND QUEENS – all tell some of the story of our past. But there is nothing like recreating the reality to bring it all vividly to life, to help us to probe beneath the surface. The Romans' horsemanship becomes more appreciable when we see re-enactors riding as they did, without stirrups. The chilliness of great castles is more immediate when we learn that the bulkiness of the medieval magnates who lived in them came at least partly from the fur linings of their clothes. Sometimes the reality may be almost too vivid – imagine the horror of having a tooth extracted without anaesthetic by a vicious pincer. We taste the blandness of a medieval poor family's bag pudding, or shy away from the lukewarm, semi-congealed food, carried through draughty corridors from distant kitchens.

Re-enactors are enthusiasts, fanatics even. They weave their own cloth, they make their own chain mail and wear it – it is *heavy* – all day in recreations of the battle of Hastings, they dress themselves and their children in clothing meticulously researched to reflect the period. Musicians make their own instruments and play authentic tunes. People cook as our ancestors would have done, using clay pots on open fires, following historical recipes and drawing on whatever ingredients would have been available. Dedicated, high-quality re-enactors are much more than entertainers; they are serious historical researchers whose work has challenged conventional opinions and thrown swathes of light on some of the facts of history. Many of them bring knowledge from disciplines other than history and archaeology to help in solving archaeologists' conundrums. Len Morgan, whose *alter ego* is the centurion Fatalis of Legio XIIII Gemina Martia Victrix, was an engineering pattern maker by trade. This experience helped him to work out many of the small details of Roman armour that had puzzled those exploring how it was made and how it worked in practice. He made his own splendid armour and weapons and now makes such items professionally for sale to other Roman re-enactors.

Re-enactment is all about authenticity – of clothing, of weapons, of methods and of historical fact. It is about studying what really happened and recreating it; changing the facts of history is not on the agenda. Re-enactment is also about joining in, whether in warfare and battles, medieval fairs or royal progresses – there is the need, and the

'You live and breathe the past at a re-enactment; it's all around you, in everything you see, hear and smell. Somehow it seems much more real than the present day.'

ABOVE: The dragon figureheads of Viking longships must have struck terror into those waiting for the raiders on shore. This elaborately carved prow featured in rowing contests at the Jorvik Viking Festival.

OPPOSITE: Examples of the varied roles open to today's re-enactors, such as medieval falconers, Tudor courtiers or World War I Tommies.

ABOVE: The Roman legionaries of Legio XX Valeria Victrix, brought to life by the Ermine Street Guard, demonstrate the menacing Roman *testudo*, or tortoise. This famous, highly disciplined formation used shields to make four walls and a roof. Under their protection, the human tank could advance despite well-armed adversaries.

BELOW: A ferocious line-up of Viking warriors, poised for the attack and armed with axes and the all-important spears. Lighter spears were designed for throwing, while heavier thrusting spears, axes, knives and swords were used at closer quarters. The Vikings' savagery and skill terrified opponents, and their charges still put spectators to instinctive flight.

room, for everyone. While one re-enactor will play William of Normandy at a recreated battle of Hastings, and someone else will take King Harold's role, there are also parts for the host of soldiers on both sides, and for women in the camps behind the lines (and, in some cases, in the thick of battle). One former re-enactor in Sir John Astley's Regimente of Foote, a Kent group devoted to the military glories of the Civil War, was known as Mistress Sladen when in a dress, but she was also a very accomplished, if unnamed, pikewoman when a soldier. As a teenager who was keen on outdoor activities, she joined because it was fun but also historically fascinating: 'Every other Sunday afternoon we'd have a skirmish … I got really good with the pike … it wouldn't have been nearly as much fun if I'd had to be a girl all the time – I liked the fighting as I was a bit of a tomboy.'

We know, of course, that it is all make-believe. While there may be hard work and discomfort, there is no blood, no death, and the most intrepid warrior will eventually go home to relax. Nevertheless, these events do bring both participants and spectators closer to understanding our forebears' lives. They offer the opportunity to try on period costume and marvel at its weight, to taste the food and pull a face, to admire the skill of cavalry and archers, musicians and storytellers. On a grander canvas, re-enactments serve to reconstruct the great battles of history that changed the world. Yet they also show what it was like to be one of the thousands of ordinary soldiers whose feudal allegiance to their masters had wrenched them away from their fields and their families, placed billhooks in their hands and lined them up as part of a steaming, shouting mass, facing tough combat and probable wounding or death.

Making a longbow and arrows

1 The bow-maker planes the wood (well-seasoned yew for the finest bows) to the correct thickness. Bows usually have two sections, jointed in the centre.

2 The planed bow stave is then bent outwards slowly by the maker. He uses a tiller, which winds an extra-strength bowstring down a series of ratchets.

3 When it reaches the correct draw for the arrows' length, the bow is strung with normal-strength bowstring made from flax or other strong thread.

4 Notches are cut in the end of the arrow to hold the flights. Arrows were made of various woods; those on the Tudor ship *Mary Rose* were of ash and poplar.

5 The flights are bound into place using strong twine. Traditional 'clothyard' arrows were 94 cm (37 in) but length varied from 76 cm (30 in) upwards.

6 Completed arrows can be fletched with various feathers, depending on the bow's purpose. Deep notches are cut in the arrows' ends for the bowstring.

Voices from the past

IT MAY SEEM ODD TO TREAT DOCUMENTS as 'living history'; are they not, after all, mere dry and dusty records – dead and worthless, not living and vibrant? Nothing could be further from the truth! They are often the closest we can get to almost hearing the voices of the past: diaries and letters, wills and census returns, newspaper cuttings and reports of trials – all imbued with the immediacy of actually *being there*.

The National Archives at Kew, near London, the new name for the combined Public Record Office and Historical Manuscripts Commission, holds documents covering 1000 years of recorded history. Its records of government contain tangible evidence of great affairs of state: Domesday Book, Magna Carta, an unbroken series of Pipe Rolls running from 1156 to 1833 (in which sheriffs accounted for revenue due to the Crown) and medieval tally sticks. Shakespeare's will and Edward VIII's 1936 letter of abdication are there, as is Guy Fawkes's signature on two confessions – the second much shakier after he had been tortured. Many of the National Archives' users, aided by the on-site bookshop, are unravelling their family history through wills, call-up papers, even accounts of trial and imprisonment. All human life is recorded in these documents, from the grandest to the most ordinary, in a unique resource that fills 167 km (103 miles) of shelves.

ABOVE AND RIGHT:
Historic documents from the National Archives connect us to the great events of the past. Both these relate to the Gunpowder Plot of 1605, when Catholic conspirators plotted to blow up the Houses of Parliament when the king, James I, was present – an event commemorated every 5 November. A list of suspects seen with one of the conspirators, Robert Catesby (above), is complemented by the confession of Guy Fawkes (right) signed after torture, with an uncharacteristically shaky hand.

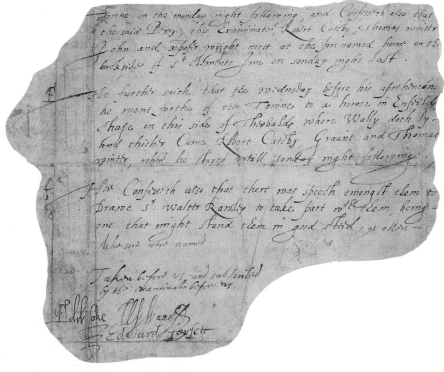

'Right worshipful brother, I recommend me to you. And as for tiding, mine Lord of York hath take mine Lord of Exeter into his award. The Duke of Somerset is still in prison, in worse case than he was ...'

WILLIAM PASTON II TO JOHN PASTON I, JULY 1454

As well as the National Archives, many other archives and libraries house Britain's written history. The British Library is the nation's major repository of private papers, including diaries and love letters. Such insights vividly evoke events and feelings of centuries ago, amplified by an awareness of all those who have handled them over the years. Hereford Cathedral's great Chained Library, the collections of Oxford's Bodleian Library and the Parker Library at Corpus Christi, Cambridge, are monuments to past lives. The Corpus Christi archive of Matthew Parker, Elizabeth I's archbishop of Canterbury, includes the Gospel believed to have been owned by St Augustine.

The very languages in which documents were written also form part of the fascination. The word 'viz', for example, meaning 'namely' or 'that is to say', comes from the Latin *videlicet*, a frequently used word often abbreviated by medieval scribes. So the 'z' at the end of the word is a medieval squiggle – a time-saving device for weary 'human photocopiers', now an established word. It is this quirky immediacy which makes documents so rewarding as a window into history.

ABOVE: A letter written to a colleague at the Great Western Railway Audit Office by a soldier on active service in 1916. Its description of the 'jolly fine life' – not yet on the front line – seems surprisingly upbeat to us, although the writer also mentions the 'live stock', presumably lice, brought back by fellow soldiers from the trenches.

RIGHT: A recreation of a casualty clearing station in World War I by the National Army Museum. The seated stretcher bearer takes a break to write home. As well as their own families, they often had to contact relatives of men who had died at the station, sending a few human details to follow the dreaded official telegram.

Getting in touch

THERE ARE SCORES OF LIVING MUSEUMS, hundreds of sites to visit, thousands of re-enactment events all over the country – so how do you find out what is available? Where do you start?

EXPLORING HISTORIC PLACES

English Heritage, Historic Scotland, Cadw (for Wales) and Manx National Heritage have a wide variety of Britain's sites and monuments in their care. Most of them are open to the public and many are free of charge; membership schemes are also very popular, offering free or discounted entry. The range of sites is enormous, from Stonehenge to Maes Howe on Orkney, from Blaenavon Ironworks to Stott Park Bobbin Mill, from the splendour of Edward I's Caernarfon Castle to the brooding majesty of Dover Castle's 2000 years of history. Find out more about them from the handbooks published by the individual organizations or from their websites. These will also give information about access for visitors with disabilities, and events and seasonal activities for children.

The National Trust and the National Trust for Scotland own and manage large numbers of historic properties in Britain, as well as great tracts of countryside and coastline. Many of the greatest houses in the country are now open to the public, often with equally magnificent

BELOW: Dover Castle on the Kent coast is one of English Heritage's flagship sites Visitors can absorb 2000 years of history, including the Roman lighthouse (just to the left of the Saxon church) and the great Norman keep (on the left of the picture). The famous white cliffs under the castle are riddled with Napoleonic tunnels, reused during World War II and converted to nuclear bunkers during the Cold War.

ABOVE: Members of the Great War Society muster at Richmond Castle in Yorkshire. They form part of the 1/8 Manchester Regiment, B Company, with their lance-corporal at the right. They wear respirators around their necks against gas attacks and the man on the left is holding a Lewis gun – the world's first effective portable machine gun.

gardens and grounds where you can enjoy the views created by owners centuries ago. Historic Royal Palaces is an organization that manages many royal buildings from Britain's past, such as the Tower of London, Hampton Court and the Banqueting House at Whitehall. The Queen's residences at Buckingham Palace and Windsor Castle are also open to the public; their handbooks or websites give details.

There are also many historic houses and monuments managed independently by their owners or trusts set up for the purpose – great houses such as Longleat, home of the Marquis of Bath with its famous wildlife park; Blenheim Palace, the family seat of the Duke of Marlborough; and Warwick Castle, managed by the Tussauds Foundation, as well as many other smaller, quirkier places. Apart from websites again, look at guides such as Hudson's *Historic Houses and Gardens* – the most comprehensive guidebook to historic places open to the public. Hudson's also currently carries a list of private houses that have received government-funded grants and so are open to the public by arrangement or on a certain number of days a year; this is the way to see some smaller gems, not easily accessible. Annual Heritage Open Days, run by the Civic Trust and funded by English Heritage, also offer hugely popular opportunities to see places, both grand and modest, not usually accessible to the public.

Guidebooks and interactive audio tours help in understanding complex or ruined sites, and offer insights into the lives of those who built and lived in them. Reading up on an attraction before a visit is a good idea, and most of the guides published by major organizations on individual sites are available by mail order. Regional guides, such as English Heritage's new series on free sites, spotlight the heritage of a particular area. Idiosyncratic tours, whether of battlefields, Blue Plaques or London and Thames valley walks 'in the footsteps of the famous', offer intriguing ways to explore historical sites.

DISCOVERING LIVING HISTORY EVENTS

English Heritage runs the biggest national programme of re-enactments and historical interpretations – about 400 a year over the summer season, ranging from full-scale battles to royal progresses, falconry and jousting to traditional country fairs and historic cricket matches. All these events are carried out by re-enactment and interpretation societies whose members research and make their own costumes and weapons, and play their roles to the full.

Re-enactment societies across Britain cover all periods and cultures, from prehistoric peoples to those of the 1950s. Their members are dedicated and passionate, eager to talk to spectators and answer questions about their historical periods and their specific roles, although they also mostly stay in character. Len Morgan becomes Fatalis for the day and requires his soldiers to seek permission before they remove their armour or go to the loo; while he is drilling his soldiers he gives commands in Latin, but he reverts to English when talking to the public and is happy to let children try on his helmet and sink under its weight. The re-enactors encourage visitors to try the food, take part in the dancing, and join in interactive story-telling.

Some societies insist on total authenticity; they take off wrist watches and refuse to eat modern food while in costume, and will not allow women to take part in military action. Other societies are less insistent and use women as pike-carriers as well as camp-followers. They take their research seriously: one member of the Medieval Siege Society, who re-enact the engagements of the Wars of the Roses, is doing a course, usually aimed at actors, on historical swordsmanship, even though his usual re-enactment role is as a crossbowman. The course is based on known and well-researched techniques written down and taught by masters of the art in the 15th century and later.

Many historical attractions regularly employ interpreters in costume to explain the history of the place to visitors; the Tower of London is one of these, as are Warwick Castle and Hampton Court. Costumed events also take place in cities and towns, such as the annual Georgian week in Tunbridge Wells. Events such as these happen across the country, ranging in scale from international occasions to intimate gatherings; the local press is the best way to hear about them. The groups who perform in them tend to see themselves as entertainers and educators rather than re-enactors, and will come out of their roles if required to answer questions or give information.

Some skilled people make their own clothes and equipment based on documents, paintings, engravings or actual examples in museums, and will then sometimes go on to sell to others; they are part of a big cottage industry, and sometimes set up their stalls at re-enactment events. But most such purchases are made at the two big fairs a year which are held in March and November, currently at the Exhibition Centre at Warwick. Everything can be bought or commissioned from specialist suppliers at these fairs, from authentic historical tents to

'As for the sounds and rhythms of medieval music, it's only rock and roll, heartbeat music … that's why audiences of all ages can clap along to the beat of a branle or a saltarello.'

BELOW: A medieval musician demonstrates how to play a 14th-century psaltery. This popular, lute-like instrument could either be played with a bow, as here, or plucked with fingers or a rudimentary plectrum.

ABOVE: The skills and dexterity of re-enactors are highly impressive. The Roman cavalry rode into battle without the aid of stirrups – tactics emulated by their modern counterparts. This cavalryman at the Roman site of Corbridge hones his combat skills on a cabbage, placed on a stand to replicate an enemy's head.

bespoke clothing, armour and weapons, and tableware and cooking equipment. Re-enactors of 20th-century battles make more use of specialist militaria suppliers who have the real thing as well as replicas. An annual magazine, *Call to Arms*, is the re-enactor's bible; it has full listings of all the companies, what they do and how they operate. Many societies have websites with information about how to join or see performances; details of several societies are given on pages 186–8.

Re-enactments are subject to health and safety regulations, as is to be expected. All societies have special insurance, members must be 16 or over, and handbooks list their various rules. Nothing sharp is allowed on a battlefield, valid targets are specified and re-enactment groups using guns need a black powder licence. The aim is to be as authentic as possible, without endangering life and limb.

VISITING LIVING HISTORY MUSEUMS

Interpreters and re-enactors are often part of living museums too, dressing in period costume to demonstrate the facets of life and work relevant to the place and time. Contact details for the living museums featured in this book are supplied on page 186; many have websites

describing the museum, together with information about opening times and costs. Most of them run special events, advertised on websites and in the local press, and many offer courses in specific historical skills. They usually run Friends schemes, and have facilities and events for schools. Some conventional museums have interactive displays and exhibitions now, so check to see what is on offer.

Living museums and open air museums can and do operate on different scales and at different levels. Some are internationally renowned, others small, local enterprises such as Gosport's Living Village of Little Woodham, which recreates the Civil War period. However, they share a close relationship with their region and subject matter. Farm animals are often traditional breeds native to the region, as at Stowmarket's Museum of East Anglian Life and the Norfolk Rural Life Museum at Gressenhall. Events reflect regional history: at Bede's World they relate to the Anglo-Saxon influence on the area in the 8th century, and include monastic skills like calligraphy. Visitors to museums of the industrial past, such as the Black Country Living Museum or Beamish, the North of England Open Air Museum, can go down mines and take trips on canal boats and steam trains. Wide-ranging activities at living museums cater for visitors' diverse interests, and often include a lot of hands-on, interactive involvement.

The establishments that combine innovative research with activities and events for visitors, such as Peat Moors, West Stow and Butser, have in part an educational approach, with excellent facilities for school parties. But they are also fun, and encourage learning through joining in traditional activities. The re-enactment group Regia Anglorum is currently constructing a living village from the 11th century at Wychurst in Kent, and welcomes both onlookers and those prepared to help. Jorvik in the city of York and West Stow Anglo-Saxon village in Suffolk are examples of living history sites that offer glimpses of past experiences in their original locations. So do the historic dockyards at Portsmouth and Chatham; their famous ships and buildings, as well as galleries such as Wooden Walls, bring past centuries to life at the places where real events happened and real history was made.

INTERPRETING DOCUMENTS

Looking at documents in the context of living history is about seeing and handling the minutiae of daily life. Letters with news of domestic events, lists of goods and chattels, account books with quantities and costs – all tell vivid and immediate stories about real events in real people's lives. And even when the event is familiar to us, such as the signed death warrant of Charles I, it is the immediacy of the signatures that brings the event closer and sends a shiver down the spine.

The National Archives in Kew holds the central government and law court documents for England and Wales, starting with Domesday Book; those of Scotland are in the National Archives of Scotland. They have huge amounts of information covering many aspects of people's lives: army service records; documents relating to crime, convicts and transportation; legal and civil action records; medieval manorial court rolls – for which a knowledge of Latin is advisable – and wills from across the centuries. To access these, simply visit with formal identification and you will be registered as a reader. It is well worth looking at the website (page 187) before visiting, as documents can be ordered in advance with reasonable notice.

Living history is about getting close, in as many ways as possible, to life in the past. It offers an imaginative, immediate and very physical experience of history. Let the last word go to one medieval re-enactor: 'It's impossible to get anywhere near the sheer brutality of real hand-to-hand combat with sharp weapons and the scent of fear in your nostrils. But you can't half get close to the smell of sweat.'

TOP AND ABOVE: A living history interpreter, enjoying royal entertainment at Bolsover Castle, has recreated Charles I's hairstyle and small pointed beard as well as his clothes (above). After the Civil War the real king was tried by Parliament and executed in January 1649; his goods and effects were inventoried and sold off by Parliament. The document listing their sale (below) dates from 1650 and is in the National Archives.

The four centuries of Roman rule in Britain imposed a new kind of society on many of its indigenous people. The Roman legions and administrators brought innovations from Mediterranean Europe: engineering skills to build roads, forts, country villas and towns;

THE ROMANS IN BRITAIN

new species of plants for food and medicine; a culture of established urban living, with schools, courts, public baths and places of entertainment. Much of the Romans' legacy remains, from communication routes and ruined buildings to onions. Yet in many rural areas life under the Romans went on much as before, dominated by the yearly farming cycle and small, local communities.

2

Approaching Roman sites

MOST OF US CAN IDENTIFY WITH THE ROMANS; we feel a sense of familiarity with their culture and way of life, which took over much of Britain for about 400 years. What they left is all around us, from their network of well-constructed, famously straight roads (many underpinning today's major arteries) to the stone foundations of our present-day towns and cities, from London to Lincoln and York, Exeter to Carlisle, Gloucester to St Albans and Colchester. In *Monty Python's Life of Brian,* John Cleese, as the leader of the ineffectual anti-Roman group, the People's Front of Judea, asks in the manner of insurgents down the centuries: 'What have the Romans ever done for us?' The answers, of course, were aqueducts, sanitation, roads, medicine, education, irrigation, public baths, public order and wine!

To the Romans, city dwelling was the root of civilization – the word itself comes from the Latin for city, *civis* – and they introduced urban living in a recognizable form to at least part of Britain. Their civic administrators and lawmakers worked out in gyms and went to saunas for socializing and relaxation, they lived in grand villas with central heating, painted plaster and nice mosaics, their sons went to

LEFT AND ABOVE: The Romans left many buildings behind them, impressive even in ruined form. One of the basilica walls at Wroxeter Roman City (left) still stands to second-storey height, and the walls at Richborough Castle (above), the Romans' base after their second invasion in AD 43, are still formidable.

school and they imported the sort of Mediterranean food – and drink – that we enjoy today. Roman structures are still linked to the fabric of today's world; we can, literally, walk in the footsteps of the Romans on their straight roads, especially in some untouched upland areas such as Wheeldale Moor where the original surface remains, and one of the Roman city gates at Lincoln remains in good repair and daily use, still negotiated by traffic after 2000 years.

We know much more about the Romans' plans, hopes and fears than those of their predecessors and immediate successors, simply because they wrote them down and much has fortuitously survived. Our modern mindset seems to relate to that of the Romans – their pragmatism, their political organization, their commercial instinct. We can also get closer to the ordinary people than ever before, because they have left their thoughts, feelings, passing comments and laments in personal letters and graffiti, and on tombstones.

They also left their ghosts. A legion of Roman soldiers has been sighted marching through the wall of a cellar at York, all mysteriously wading through the floor at knee-height. Later investigations revealed that a Roman road existed on the site, its level well beneath the surface of the modern cellar's floor.

ABOVE: The Romans built magnificent villas in their new province, both in towns and the surrounding countryside. Many have been excavated and elaborate mosaic floors revealed. This stalking leopard is from the Great Pavement at Woodchester, one of the most intricate mosaics in northern Europe.

Visiting Roman sites

Atmospheric Roman sites exist in many parts of Britain, reflecting the skill and energy of their engineers, builders and craftsmen. Some are still impressive even in a ruined state – the magnificent public baths at Aquae Sulis (Bath), elaborate country villas at Chedworth, Lullingstone, Bignor and Fishbourne, the mighty Saxon Shore forts, built late in Roman times to withstand the new invaders from the European north, and the great Roman camps at Caerleon and on Hadrian's Wall. Others are smaller and more intimate, such as the remains of a small Roman bath complex in one of Glasgow's suburbs. And these sites are peopled: gravestones, graffiti, domestic and personal objects all tell us about the long-gone men, women and children whose homes and places of work these were. They offer a direct link with the Romans and the Britons who were here, helping re-enactors to discover what they – and their lives – were really like.

TOP: Hadrian's Wall, stretching from Wallsend on the River Tyne to the Solway Firth, is an impressive feat of Roman engineering. Delineated in snow (top), it powerfully conveys how bleak and desolate the posting must have been for legionaries from all over the empire who served here.

ABOVE: The wall and its fortresses were built by the legions of Chester, Caerleon and York, and garrisoned by auxiliary troops. Modern re-enactment groups such as the Ermine Street Guard (above) regularly use the site to demonstrate their armour, weapons and authentic military techniques.

The legacy of the legions

The Romans came to conquer, and everywhere the armies went they built strongly fortified camps, often within the large enclosed settlements already in existence. The legions' progress into the north, centre and west of Britain was marked by their trademark rectangular forts, easily defended and quickly dominating the landscape. They remain today in various guises: some, especially early structures made from timber and earth, are now visible only as cropmarks in fields, and many others are buried in the foundations of later settlements. Others are still prominent: the ditches at Richborough, Kent – the

LEFT: Legio XX Valeria Victrix drill and parade at Corbridge, displaying their painstakingly manufactured *lorica segmentata* and helmets. The Roman army recruited young men from all over the empire, offering good pay and pensions, in the form of land grants, if they survived 25 years' service.

ABOVE: A *pugio*, or dagger, was carried by all legionaries for close-quarter fighting. As with the *gladius*, or short stabbing sword, the idea was to stab rather than slash. The point had only to penetrate a short way into a vulnerable spot to maim or kill.

Romans' landing place in Britain in AD 43 – are still formidably deep, and the Roman fort wall and towers at Pevensey still stand to virtually their full height, 1700 years after construction. The Roman lighthouse, technology new to Britain, still stands on the heights at Dover – a hugely important strategic position that rightly boasts its 2000 years of history and its role as the gateway of England.

Hadrian's Wall is perhaps their most magnificent monument, snaking for more than 112 km (70 miles) across the beautiful but often inhospitable Scottish borders. Built, in the words of Hadrian's biographer, to separate the Romans from the Barbarians, the wall retains its original height in some places and is a regular magnet for walkers. Many of the Romans' permanent forts on the wall are still there, ruined but still splendid. At Housesteads on a winter's day it is all too easy to imagine how bleak and unforgiving this posting would have seemed to a soldier from one of the warmer parts of the empire, some of whom certainly served here. Once the new province was settled, auxiliary regiments drew upon local recruits in their line-up, but they were always still commanded by Roman citizens, many of them men of rank in their own countries serving a stint in the Roman army as a route to status and wealth. Several of these officers have left their names behind, as well as clues to their feelings about serving in Britain. Gaius Cornelius Peregrinus, serving in Cumbria, dedicated an altar to the 'Genius of Place, Fortune who brings men home'; he was clearly missing the warmth of Mauretania, his North African home. The climate also brought physical problems, such as the lack of vitamin D from the sun, which caused particular problems for soldiers from warmer lands serving in the chilly north. In some respects, however, military life in the vast fortresses – many of them bigger than the new towns – was relatively comfortable; a Roman soldier's room was, on average, bigger than that allocated to a 19th-century British one. Health and hygiene were catered for, as shown by the communal lavatory at Housesteads. However, excavation has also revealed less salubrious quarters where insect infestations indicate a build-up of dirt that would have made for a rather squalid home. Then as now, perhaps, some people were cleaner than others.

The damp conditions that would have depressed the soldiers have nevertheless improved our knowledge of their lives, by preserving thin wooden writing tablets from the Roman fort at Vindolanda. These provide fascinating insight into life in the camp; one records a soldier's request for warm socks and underwear; another is a shopping list and a third is an invitation from one woman asking another to her birthday party – direct and immediate links to real people leading real lives 2000 years ago. Some of these lives were abruptly cut short, as is revealed by graves, their markers and other kinds of inscription. A tribune at Birdoswald on Hadrian's Wall mourned for his little son

LEFT: Remains of the bath house at Vindolanda on Hadrian's Wall, site of a Roman army fort and an adjacent *vicus*, or town. Roman baths, using a central heating system of furnace and hypocausts (hot air vents), were an essential part of military and civilian life.

BELOW: A Roman shopping list from Vindolanda features bruised beans, 20 chickens, 100 apples, fish sauce and olives, and asks for all to be purchased at a fair price. Other 'Vindolanda tablets', written on wood and preserved in a waterlogged rubbish dump, offer further insights into daily life. They include a birthday party invitation and requests for warm underwear.

ABOVE AND LEFT:
Hadrian's Wall itself forms one of the sides of Housesteads Roman Fort, the best preserved of the wall forts. Its typical rectangular design is clearly visible in this aerial photograph (above). The legionary (left) is wearing a reconstructed helmet of the 1st century AD; its almost horizontal rear neck guard is typical of this period.

'We're building a hypocaust to find out how they really worked ... how the Romans managed to force hot air along a horizontal passage without losing it upwards.'

(VOLUNTEER AT BUTSER)

who lived 'one year and five days'; how poignant is that exact measurement of so short a life. Another soldier, Aurelius Marcus, mourned for his 'very pure wife who lived 33 years without blemish'; and another grave marker from South Shields tells us in very few words a great deal both about the family it commemorates and the realities of life on the wall:

> *Regina Liberta et Coniuge*
> *Barates Palmyrensis natione*
> *Catuellauna an xxx*

This translates as 'Regina, freedwoman and wife of Barates of Palmyra, of the Catuvellauni, died aged 30'. Underneath, in the Palmyric language, is written 'Regina, the freedwoman of Barates, alas'. We know that Barates was a trader because his own, much simpler, tombstone has also been found; it therefore seems that he came all the way from Palmyra in Syria to trade at the frontier of the Roman Empire, took a slave girl from an indigenous tribe, freed and married her; that sad little word 'alas' indicates that he also loved her and mourned her death. And does the fact that he added to the inscription

ABOVE: A Roman curse tablet retrieved from the sacred spring at Bath. Petitioners scratched their messages on to sheets of pewter, invoking divine power to solve the intrigues and petty crimes of daily life. Many complained of clothing stolen while using the baths, and the tablet of one unfortunate man records the loss of both tunic and cloak.

'Roman women loved jewellery – rich necklaces made from gold, amber and jet, rings on every finger … Brooches were practical, too, fastening tunics at the shoulders. It can be hard to get the tunic to drape properly, but when it does the folds are very flattering.'

ABOVE: A Roman woman wearing a tunic, pinned on both shoulders with ornate brooches, and a simple bead necklace. Her hair is fastened back in a style recognizable from grave markers and portrait heads. Women often contribute to Roman re-enactments by demonstrating typical foods and cooking techniques, as well as the fashions and craft activities of the time.

in his native language indicate feelings of nostalgia for his birthplace and homesickness? It is these small, endlessly fascinating signatures, mysterious as they are, that draw us closer to people such as Barates and Regina, who lived nearly two millennia ago.

ROMAN URBAN LIFE

As soon as the Romans were militarily secure in Britain, they started to build towns. Many are still important centres today, their ancient foundations long obscured by 2000 years of development. Others, such as Silchester in Hampshire and Wroxeter in Shropshire, have not been built over since they were abandoned. Roman Silchester's walls and embankments now defend acres of farmland within which the ghostly shapes of streets and buildings are clearly visible in aerial photographs. Wroxeter also contains Roman shops; in one of them, a stack of samian bowls was found toppled over, lying nested together just as they had fallen 1800 years ago during a fire in the forum in about AD 170. We can only wonder what happened to the shopkeeper and why he abandoned his stock of expensive tableware where it fell.

The superstructures of Roman buildings have mostly long gone, but their underpinnings often remain: the hypocausts to provide that early, efficient form of central heating, so necessary for those used to heat and sun; the water and drainage systems essential for that centrepiece of Mediterranean life, the public baths. At Bath, the Roman city of Aquae Sulis, the reservoir and great drain have yielded up huge quantities of objects thrown in as petitions: a gold earring, an inlaid brooch, many metal vessels, a bag containing 33 beautifully engraved gemstones, and thousands of coins. These were valuable objects: four of the coins were gold, two months' salary for an official of rank. The need for divine help must have been great indeed.

Hundreds of curse tablets were also discovered, written on pewter and rolled up before being consigned to the magic waters. Many of them ask the goddess to wreak her vengeance on miscreants, written ritualistically, hedging bets in all directions, and listing the people who may be responsible. One Annianus had had six silver pieces stolen from his purse, and cited 18 suspects, requesting that the goddess would investigate them all 'whether pagan or Christian, whether man or woman, whether boy or girl, whether slave or free'. Another records a family who were in dispute: all had sworn at the spring on 12 April, and the goddess would be able to know which one of them was lying.

Formal histories seldom bother with these small incidents of daily life, but they offer insights into real people with problems and issues, many similar to those we experience now.

There is a great deal of Roman material to be seen and touched in the bathing complex: visitors can still walk in the footsteps of the Romans on an original Roman pavement and their lead pipes are *in situ* and in use. You can look through the original Roman arches into the reservoir fed by the sacred spring, which delivers 1,170,000 litres of hot mineral water a day. The water level is the same as in Roman times, and although there is no longer a roof and the statues on plinths reaching just to the water's surface have gone, on a cold day it is steamy and atmospheric, evoking a space that must have seemed god-like and mysterious for Roman petitioners. The Great Bath's fabric is also Roman, though its superstructure is Victorian. No one can bathe here today, as the Romans would have done, but the curative water can be drunk from a water pump in the Pump Rooms.

The healing properties of the hot waters were greatly needed. Not only was the death rate high and age at death frequently very young, but excavations of cemeteries have revealed that practically everyone who lived past the age of 30 suffered from osteoarthritis, and lead poisoning was endemic. Eye problems, particularly conjunctivitis, appear to have been very common, if the number of patent medicines on sale for these problems are an indication; deficiencies in diet are likely to have been the cause.

ABOVE: One of Butser's several roundhouses, based on the archaeological remains found at Moel y Gerddi, Carmarthenshire. Hazel rods are used in the wattle and daub walls and the roof is thatched with locally grown wheat straw, producing a well insulated, waterproof building. Unusually, it has two doors opposite one another, facing southeast (as shown) and northwest. A log pile is stored in the shelter of the roof.

BELOW: The interior of the Moel y Gerddi roundhouse is dominated by the central hearth, which would have provided a social and practical focus for people living there. Experiments have shown clearly that that smoke simply dispersed through the thatch; a specific smoke vent would have acted as a funnel and drawn the fire upwards, risking a blaze. The iron cooking pot is suspended by an iron chain, drawing on evidence of remnants found in excavated hearth areas.

OPPOSITE: Butser Ancient Farm in Hampshire, with its constructs of different sized roundhouses, tests archaeological theories by trial and error, usually over long periods. The houses' circular design has proved remarkably robust; a rectangular porch over the doorway of one was destroyed in a recent storm while the round thatched roof was unaffected. The steep pitch of the thatch (an angle of 45°) proved the most successful in allowing rain to drain away.

COUNTRY LIVING

The cities were new to the indigenous people, although some were built on the sites of earlier tribal settlements. Much of the Romans' new province remained rural and agricultural, producing the food and other supplies vital for the legions and urban dwellers. For many Britons, especially those in remote areas, the coming of the Romans would have had little impact. The pattern of existence was still dominated by seasons and the vagaries of the weather. There was plenty of food to be had in the summer, particularly after the harvest had restocked the grain stores, while winter required the stockpiling and storage of food through the traditional preservation techniques of salting, drying and smoking. Much of Britain had been farmed productively before the Romans arrived and this continued for centuries, with the farmers paying the Romans' taxes in grain.

Much of our knowledge of rural life and agricultural practices in the Iron Age and Roman periods derives from experimental archaeology, which explores the problems and questions that archaeology raises through direct experience. Butser Ancient Farm in Hampshire is an 'open air laboratory', dedicated to exploring the practical realities of the past. Grain pits dug there, for example, have proved that grain could be successfully stored throughout the winter, providing the ingredients for bread to stave off famine in the year's dark, lean months. Teams at Butser have also managed to keep grain dry and safe from rodents by constructing effective above-ground grain stores – the usual interpretation for the four- and six-post buildings regularly found at settlements of this period. The farm grows authentic varieties of crops in prehistoric field systems, harvested with authentic tools, and keeps breeds of animals, such as the Soay sheep from St Kilda, that are as close as possible to their ancient forebears. Butser also has some of the ancient Manx Loghtan breed of sheep, now being farmed again on the Isle of Man. Its meat is available by mail order, but the farmer warns that its taste is quite different from modern lamb; he suggests mint sauce would not be appropriate!

Butser features several constructs of roundhouses, based on archaeological discoveries of rings of posts with a burnt area in the middle. The Peat Moors Centre on the Somerset Levels also contains reconstructions of Iron Age roundhouses, drawing on archaeological evidence from excavations on Glastonbury's 'Lake Village'. Inside are hearths, cooking pots, weapons, furs and simple furniture, and it is possible to imagine living there in surprising comfort. Smoke from the hearths, for example, disperses quite easily into the circular roofs. The Peat Moors buildings use the ancient technique of wattle and daub (a mix of clay, dung and chopped straw) for their walls; they are thatched with reeds, still growing locally.

The constructs of such ancient buildings are based on ground plan evidence only – often no more than post- or stake-holes and gullies. (There were 13 mounds at the Peat Moors site, for example, and another 74 at the Glastonbury 'Lake Village'.) They are informed guesswork, tested throughout a lengthy lifespan in use and in decay. If the ideas ultimately turn out to be wrong, it does not necessarily mean failure – the information is still valuable. A recreation of an Iron Age house from Pimperne in Dorset, for example, did not develop the sort of gully under the eaves that archaeologists had presumed resulted from rain dripping off the roof. However, rodent activity did produce a gully between the stakes in the outer wall of the house.

Roundhouses are usually linked to the Iron Age, but many country people would have lived in similar dwellings right through the Roman period. Pieces of Roman pottery from Chysauster in Cornwall have been associated with roundhouses that had been there for centuries; their stone foundations, opening on to courtyards with worn paving slabs, can still be visited, although the patterns of adjacent Iron Age fields have now been destroyed.

The practical crafts and techniques of rural life hardly changed for centuries. The Peat Moors Centre in Somerset has a reconstructed Romano-British kiln where pottery is fired in traditional ways. Bronze casting and iron smelting also take place on the site, as well as spinning, dyeing and woodwork, all using authentic tools such as a foot-driven lathe. The centre also grinds its own corn, which is then baked into loaves in a bread oven. Butser also features these activities.

A major innovation by the Romans was the building of villas in the countryside. They were the centres of large agricultural estates, and even the smallest of them were luxurious dwellings, with hypocausts, mosaics and painted walls; many of them had their own bath houses too. These villas were often near towns, which may indicate that their owners also had urban interests. A current experiment at Butser is a construct of a Roman villa, designed to test how the hypocaust actually works. Building methods are being rigorously tested as the experiment progresses.

'It's almost magical to build or make something with replicas of ancient tools and techniques, and to see it really take shape and work. You can make a pot and cook in it over an open fire in a thatched roundhouse, and even eat it without your eyes streaming from the smoke – it really does drift out through the thatch.'

BELOW: The interior of this roundhouse at the Peat Moors Centre draws on evidence from Mound 74 at Glastonbury's Iron Age 'Lake Village'. It contains replica Iron Age equipment, including a typical tripod stool by the hearth and a weaving frame leaning against the wall. Life in the more remote and rural areas of Britain continued relatively unchanged by the Roman administration.

ABOVE: Living history interpreters at the Peat Moors settlement undertake a variety of practical Iron Age skills. Here they demonstrate (from left to right) building a wattle and daub wall; planing wood on a shave-horse; weaving wool on a wooden loom; moulding clay pots, to be fired in Iron Age and Roman kilns; and spinning wool by hand. Their authentic dress reflects the colourful and boldly patterned clothing of the Iron Age and Roman centuries.

The Roman villa at Fishbourne, West Sussex, is one of the most magnificent ever found, although it dates from the early years of the Roman presence. It is traditionally associated with Cogidubnus, a native prince who clearly embraced Roman ways with enthusiasm, and a certain lack of foresight. Many of the rooms in the early villa had no provision for heating – evidence of the design's Mediterranean origins – and the floors were damaged by braziers dragged in later for warmth. The villa boasted several gardens, including a central formal garden where Roman bedding trenches, visible as dark lines in the subsoil, were discovered and replanted with box. There is also a recreated Roman potting shed, complete with tools, and a kitchen garden has been found, conveniently close to the ovens and protected from salt-laden winds. There is little evidence yet of the plants in these gardens, but preserved organic matter may yield clues in the future.

Recreating the past

'*We're lucky, in Legio XIII, to have a centurion's grave stele which gives the design of our shields; we still have to guess the colours, though …*'

ABOVE: Each century, or unit, of the Roman legion carried its *signum* (standard) while on a march or campaign. This one is likely to be the standard of the first century of the two-century maniple, shown by the hand; the wreath probably indicates an award.

OPPOSITE: Faces of the Roman legions: military re-enactment of the period involves a fascinating variety of headgear. Transverse plumes (centre top and bottom) were worn by centurions, making them obvious to their men as they led from the front in battle.

ROMAN FORTS, ROADS AND VILLAS offer a fascinating backdrop for living history interpretations. Authentic costumes, behaviour and settings are as important as in later centuries to those discovering what it was really like to be a Roman soldier shivering on guard duty on Hadrian's Wall or fired up with adrenalin in battle, to wear a toga or, for a woman, to have her hair dressed in the Roman manner by slaves, or to cook and eat Roman food. Through making and wearing the clothes and the armour, through marching and drilling, through domestic chores and elaborate feasts, both re-enactors and spectators can get an inkling of what it was like to live in Roman Britain.

BRINGING THE LEGIONS TO LIFE

Excavations at Corbridge, on Hadrian's Wall, in 1964 turned up a blacksmith's hoard of pieces of armour and other metal objects, neatly packed into a wooden crate and buried in about AD 130. This hoard revealed a great deal about the types and designs of the Romans' armour, particularly body armour (*lorica segmentata*) – an ingenious arrangement of leather straps and iron segments that was both effective and flexible. The discovery allowed much more accurate reconstruction, quickly exploited by the Roman military re-enactment groups who recreate the legions' presence in Britain. They often use sites that the Romans themselves would have known: Richborough, site of the landing in AD 43; Pevensey, which they defended towards the end of their occupation against Saxon incursions; and most of all Hadrian's Wall, both an amazing feat of engineering and an acknowledgement of military limits. The Ermine Street Guard are frequently to be seen at Fishbourne Roman Palace in Sussex, demonstrating battle tactics and showing onlookers how to march and throw a spear.

The overwhelming strength and near-invincibility of the Roman army lay in its iron discipline and its rigorous systems of training and routine. Their terrifying battle tactics included powerful formations such as the famous *testudo,* the tortoise, when a unit of soldiers would throw their shields over their heads and round their sides to form an armoured box within which to advance against the enemy. The effectiveness of this forerunner of the tank was enhanced by the Roman habit of using the sword to stab rather than to slash. They only needed to leave a chink of space between their shields to use their swords, and the sword only had to penetrate a few centimetres into

the opposing soldier's torso to wound or kill. How terrifying this must have been to opponents unaccustomed to discipline or teamwork in battle, relying instead on individual acts of strength and valour.

Roman horsemanship was awesome – and today's cavalry are as magnificent as their Roman forebears, riding into their mock battles as the Romans did, without the support of stirrups. Re-enactors carry the full weight of Roman armour and weaponry: the iron helmet, often with a crest dyed in a variety of colours for easy identification during a battle; the *lorica segmentata*; the short stabbing sword and the sharp javelins; and the large, semi-cylindrical shield decorated with the legion's insignia. Many re-enactors make their own armour if they have the skills, but others buy it at re-enactment fairs or commission it from professional historical armourers. The colours of the insignia are not easy to research, though the designs can sometimes be found on grave markers from all over the Roman empire. Legions sometimes stayed in one place for several years, but they could also be posted anywhere in the Roman world, and so evidence from across the empire can be used to help in the hunt for authenticity.

The centurion Fatalis of the Roman Military Research Society, is (living) proof of this in the form of his modern *alter ego*, Len Morgan. The members of this re-enactment group have chosen to reconstitute themselves as Legio XIIII Gemina Martia Victrix, who were the conquerors of Boudicca in AD 61 and known thereafter as 'Domitores Britannorum' – the Tamers of the Britons. The Society models itself on the legion as it was constituted slightly later, during the reign of the Emperor Trajan, and they make all their own armour and weapons. Their drill commands and invocations are in Latin, and each soldier takes the name of a real, known member of the legion. Fatalis, who wears a helmet with a transverse crest so that his soldiers can see and follow him in battle, is known to have served in many campaigns, both in Britain and elsewhere in the empire. He died in Palestine where his gravestone has been found, dedicated by his wife Vednica, a freed slave, with the words 'May the earth lie lightly on your bones'. In his current incarnation, he is an impressive and authoritative figure who would have been terrifying to the enemy and a formidable officer to his men; but he is also willing to demonstrate the excellent design of the openwork Roman sandal, which laces right down to the toes and would have allowed the wearing of several pairs of socks to combat the cold and damp. He also recounts the story of a march for

'The lorica's *a lot like a jacket and, though it's tight round the body, it's quite comfortable and not too heavy. At least you can still move around easily.'*

OPPOSITE: Standards were icons of a legion's prowess, and also marked unit positions during an engagement. Standard bearers and trumpeters wore wolf- or bearskins (shown here at Corbridge) as a high-profile badge of office. The skins are often those of animals culled in Canada, though some American re-enactors of the Roman period wear the skin of a coyote.

BELOW: Officers and men of all ranks are needed to create an authentic legion. The *optio*, second-in-command of a century, is distinguished by his staff and ring.

charity down a Roman road in Wales, during which re-enactors wearing Roman sandals suffered far fewer blisters than modern soldiers in their leather boots.

The writings of the Roman historian Tacitus, son-in-law of Agricola (Britain's governor from AD 78 to 84), give a great deal of information about the legions in the 1st century AD. His accounts show how they consolidated their military presence in what must have initially seemed a very distant and inhospitable land – all very useful for re-enactors seeking authentic details of the past. Roman legionaries had to be Roman citizens, and were professionals who spent most of their active lives in the army. The men serving in Britain in the decades after the invasion were therefore mostly soldiers from the older empire: they included Italians, Thracians, North Africans, Germans and many other nationalities.

Roman citizens also commanded the auxiliary regiments, which non-Roman citizens could join. Eventually, when Britain was regarded as settled, they included local recruits in their line-up. This mixed bag of nationalities means that re-enactors can legitimately choose from a wide variety of different customs, cultures, languages and dress.

Arming a Roman legionary

1 The various pieces of armour and weaponry used by a legionary of the 1st and 2nd centuries AD. They include the breastplate, particularly useful against slashing or piercing weapons, the helmet and metal apron, together with the *gladius* (sword), spear and large rectangular shield.

2 The ingenious breastplate, known as the *lorica segmentata*, is placed over a linen or woollen undershirt. The *lorica segmentata* fits snugly and weighs as little as 5.5 kg. It is designed to be flexible and give protection without constricting the movement so important in the thick of battle.

3 The breastplate fastens down the front with strong leather laces. It can be put on and taken off easily, but re-enactors often help each other to avoid over-stressing the surprisingly fragile straps, hinges and buckles. Later versions used hooks and eyes to simplify construction and assembly.

4 The metal apron is buckled on to the belt at the front. It was intended to be more a decorative than a protective cover, although it might also have offered some cover for the genitals. The *gladius*, a short stabbing sword, is worn on the right hip, and the helmet added to complete the ensemble.

5 Fully armed with spear and shield, the legionary was a formidable opponent who fought as part of an efficient machine. The devices on the shields relate to particular legions; they are reconstructed from grave markers and other carvings, though colours have to be deduced or guessed at.

The auxiliary commanders were usually men of rank in their own countries, since service in the army was an attractive career option for the empire's ambitious young men. And even in this far-flung corner of the empire, there were direct links with Rome: one cavalry commander serving here was awarded the senatorial toga and embarked on a political career; while one woman, Iulia Lucilla, made sure that her status as the daughter of a senator was made clear on her husband's gravestone. Soldiers were well paid, particularly the senior officers, and most of those who survived would eventually have enjoyed a comfortable and wealthy retirement, augmented by grants of land. Their pay was banked for them in the camp strongholds, after stoppages for food and clothing, and they often supplemented their supplies from the rest of their pay.

Many of the soldiers formed lasting relationships and – later, when it was permitted – marriages, which means that there are plenty of roles for women and children in authentic re-enactments. We know about many of these relationships from tombstones: one states that Julius Valens, who had served in the Second Legion at Caerleon, was buried at the age of 100 by his wife and son; the son later buried his mother, who lived to be 75. Such longevity was unusual, however, in times when both disease and military action could be perilous. An

ABOVE: A *cornucen* rallies the troops at a Roman military re-enactment. The *cornu*, or *cornum*, was a large coiled horn or trumpet, carried over the shoulders when a legion was on the march. The *cornucen* himself had to be visible to his legion, and was distinguished by his wolf- or bearskin headgear.

RIGHT: When the Roman legions left Britain in the 5th century, Saxon incursions in the east and south increased. In this re-enactment at Richborough, one of the Saxon Shore forts, invaders are confronted by Romano-British defenders. The Saxon forces had the best of it.

ABOVE: Roman chariot races at Kirby Hall, Northamptonshire. Such chariots were used for sport in the Roman amphitheatres and places of entertainment built across the new province. Hooliganism and street fights were common at chariot races, as gangs of supporters cheered on their teams.

BELOW: Athletic Romano-British and Saxon warriors really enter into the spirit of the battle at Richborough. Hand-to-hand combat, even with blunt swords, offers the opportunity for real experiment with weapons and tactics, and cuts and bruises are frequently part of a re-enactor's life.

epidemic may have carried off the wife, mother-in-law and six-year-old son of Julius Maximus, who was stationed at Ribchester. And there was violence too: the skeletons of a man and woman were found under a building near the gateway of the fort at Housesteads, presumably murdered and concealed; one wonders whether the crime and its perpetrators were ever discovered.

FASHION AND COSMETICS

Grave markers, perhaps surprisingly, are an important source of information about Roman fashions. Hairstyles – elaborate and simple – can be recreated from the images carved on them. More direct, if rather macabre, evidence comes from an excavation in York, where a Roman woman's body was found complete with hair, arranged in a bun and held with jet pins. Cosmetics and perfumes can sometimes be reconstituted from residues in the pots that contained them, such as a mixture of animal fat, lavender and sandalwood found in a flagon. Some of them would have been a severe danger to health, such as the

lead used in preparations designed to whiten skin. Spots, like today, were deplored; Ovid has a recipe against them, but also, more realistically, suggested powdering over them. He also gives a recipe for a skin toner made of poppies pounded in water, and a facepack of honey, egg and oatmeal – both rather modern sounding. And there is evidence that Roman women shaved or otherwise depilated their legs and armpits. Indeed, shaving for both men and women was a painful process involving lots of cuts; Martial warned against one particular barber, Antiocus, who was more than usually inept, and Pliny the Elder gives a recipe involving spiders' webs mixed with oil and vinegar to staunch the blood. There was, it seems, widespread relief among men when Hadrian started a fashion for beards. More painfully, hairs were sometimes plucked out individually; Seneca, who lived above a baths in Rome, was disturbed by 'the screams of those who were having their armpits plucked'.

Grave markers can also tell us a lot about dress. Men and women both wore tunics, belted at the waist with a blouson effect, but those worn by women were usually longer. The letter found at Vindolanda from a soldier asking for warm socks and underwear indicates that they would have worn underpants or loincloths. Residues of linen and silk have been found, but the most common material for clothing was wool. Buttons had not been invented so clothes were fastened with

ABOVE: Makers of equipment for re-enactments provide everything that can possibly be needed, including leather tents. This one is based on fragments of a goatskin tent found at Vindolanda, which probably belonged to the centurion.

Making a Roman sandal

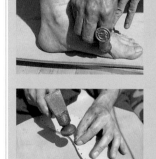   

1 A foot is used to make a template for the sandal's size and shape. The template is then cut out and tacked on to a large leather sheet.

2 The foot covering is scored into a large number of strips. The strips let the sandal adjust to the individual foot, making it very flexible to wear.

3 Laces are added to bind the strips. Roman sandals could be unlaced to the toe, allowing the wearer to put on several socks in cold weather.

4 The finished sandal: comfortable and very hard-wearing on long marches. Studs on the sole, however, need constant maintenance.

'I've marched 100 miles in these sandals, and ended up with fewer blisters than modern soldiers in proper army boots.'

ABOVE: A soldier relaxes with a meal outside his leather tent, his *gladius* still at the ready. Grains rather than meat were the mainstay of the soldiers' diet, and coarse breads with a high bran content were known as 'common' or 'army' bread. Dairy products (except butter), fish, poultry and many other birds were eaten, but beef was a rarity.

ties and thongs, or pinned with brooches, of which large numbers of different styles and fashions have been found in excavations. The grave marker of a smith shows him wearing a tunic with one shoulder left bare to allow his right arm greater freedom of movement. In contrast, a whole family in York is depicted wearing heavy, all-encompassing clothes against the cold. Although some soldiers wore knee breeches, trousers were generally regarded as unsophisticated and they remained the clothing of the un-Romanized Britons.

Tacitus tells us that part of the Romanizing of the British resulted in togas being seen everywhere; yet there are few depictions from Roman Britain of anyone wearing a toga, and several Roman emperors issued edicts enforcing its use as a formal garment. Just why this was necessary is shown by attempts to wear one properly: it is a clumsy piece of clothing, a nuisance to drape properly, and heavy and cumbersome to wear; it requires its wearer to walk in a slow and dignified manner, which is presumably why people rushing about their daily business preferred something lighter and more convenient. Its value as an indication of 'Roman-ness' might soon have palled when the problems of wearing it every day became apparent; though its weight and warmth might have been more attractive in the cold north than in the heat of Rome. A tunic was usually worn underneath.

THE ROMAN PALATE

Evidence for the food eaten in Roman Britain comes from a number of sources: bones and other remains found in excavations; depictions of food, feasts and hunting on mosaics, pottery and wall paintings; the Vindolanda tablets, several of which list the foods the writer has eaten; and literature, including the cookery book written by Apicius.

Of course, the Roman incomers utilized the food already available. Beef, pork and chicken, fish and shellfish were all staples; British oysters, highly prized, were exported to Rome, and millions of their shells have been found at Roman sites. But they also introduced a great many new plants and animals into the British diet, many of which have remained staples ever since. Pheasants and guinea fowl were Roman innovations, as were the cabbages, lettuces and turnips that they planted among other new vegetables, as well as onions and garlic. Roman influence greatly widened the range of herbs used, introducing such basics as parsley, mint, thyme, rosemary and sage. A shop in Colchester that was burnt down during Boudicca's rebellion had stocked dill, coriander, aniseed, celery seed and poppy seed. Honey was the only sweetener, but flavourings, such as pepper, ginger and cinnamon, were imported in large quantities. So were olives, olive oil, almonds, dates and wine. Hundreds of the amphorae in which they were transported have been found, many with evidence of their contents: one from the Thames contained thousands of olive pips; another found on Hadrian's Wall was marked as containing wine mixed with horehound, a cough cure; while many others held wine of varying quality (the Romans failed to acquire a taste for native British beer).

Fish sauce is one Roman ingredient that seems strange to modern tastes – until, perhaps, we think of Chinese beef in oyster sauce or the fish sauce common in Thai cooking. The famous *garum* or *liquamen*, made from fermented fish entrails, was an essential ingredient in Roman cooking, used in both sweet and savoury dishes. Fish entrails and salt were put in a pot and left out in the sun for two months, with frequent shaking; it was then strained for the resulting liquor. Another method involved boiling the fish in strong brine – tested by throwing an egg into it to see if it floated – in a pot with oregano, then allowing it to cool and straining it several times. Modern recreations tend to

ABOVE: Fish sauce, made from fermented entrails and added to a wide variety of dishes, was one of the staples of Roman cooking. This fragment of an amphora, found recently at Carlisle, still – very unusually – has clay panels with writing in ink describing its contents: 'Tunny fish relish from Tangiers, old … for the larder … excellent … top quality.'

LEFT: Authentic Roman food cooked at the Richborough Roman Festival includes stuffed kidneys, spicy sausages, bread and cheese bread. Cooks tend to use anchovy essence or Thai fish sauce in their recreated dishes, but stick to the flavourings and ingredients that the Romans would have had available in this country.

'Sausages haven't changed all that much, to judge from the Roman ones I tried today – though only if the modern ones you buy are the really good, meaty ones.'

ABOVE: Craft activities at Roman living history events include calligraphy, using parchment rolls, ink and recreated reed pens that resemble those the Romans would have known. The writing on the scroll above is in Greek. Literacy in Greek was a mark of prestige among educated, cultured Romans, and today's re-enactment societies often include similarly skilled scribes.

use anchovy essence, though some diehards make the original and cook with it. Sosia Juncina, a member of the Roman Military Research Society, has written her own cookbook and puts on displays of Roman food at their re-enactments; she makes her own fish sauce which, she says, even her cats won't go near.

Roman living history events frequently include demonstrations of food and cooking. Re-enactors at Fishbourne regularly hold Roman culinary evenings, cooking authentic food and publishing the recipes on their website. Visiting school parties work as slaves in the kitchen for the day, grinding corn and making bread. Most households ground their own flour to make bread, formed into dense, flat loaves; they also made cheese, which was eaten with bread or sliced in salads.

In many ways Roman Britain was an interlude: they came, stayed for a while and left. Living history brings us closer to those remarkable centuries before tribal, rural ways of life resumed, and to the lawgivers and legionaries, traders and slaves who shaped the Roman province.

For centuries after the Roman legions left Britain, life was precarious and uncertain. As towns and villa estates crumbled, new settlers from Europe – Angles, Saxons, Jutes and Franks – brought a pagan warrior culture to eastern and southern Britain.

SAXONS, VIKINGS & NORMANS

Gradually towns developed and Christianity was revived, but most people remained farmers, working the land. Viking raiders from Denmark and Norway terrorized coastal regions, destroying crops and colonizing whole areas. A Saxon aristocracy flourished in the 11th century, but the Norman victory at Hastings heralded a new, often brutal era for rich and poor alike.

3

Approaching Saxon, Viking and Norman times

FROM THE FINAL COLLAPSE OF ROMAN RULE IN 410, through the migrations and settlement of Saxons, Jutes, Angles and Franks, to the brutality of the Norman incursion in 1066, these six centuries are in some ways harder to reach than those before and after them. From a modern perspective they appear turbulent times of battles and invasions, in which a pagan culture celebrated warriors above all else. The term 'Dark Ages' conjures up images of primitive communities living in perpetual fear, enlivened only by feasts and stories of Beowulf told on stormy nights in mead halls.

Such a view has elements of truth. The 5th and 6th centuries were indeed periods of migrations and incursions, when life's harshness and unpredictability forced people back towards a pre-Roman, tribal existence. Civilization in the Roman sense seems to have fragmented with surprising rapidity; most towns were abandoned and hillforts re-occupied. The legend of King Arthur, stripped of medieval trappings, has its origins in this period. He is a misty figure, thought to have been a Romano-British warlord, leading resistance as Anglo-Saxons pressed deeper into the centre and west of Britain. Kings and nobles of the time acquired and held on to power through sheer force of arms. Their exploits were celebrated in ballads, they were the heroes of the sagas, and they bore magnificently decorated weapons, helmets and shields.

Despite recurring conflict, the main concern of most people was the need to grow, harvest and store food. Anglo-Saxon villages like West Stow and Mucking were communities of farmers and craftsmen skilled in crafts such as metal- and woodwork. Many incomers brought their families to settle, and in time Saxon kings established the fortified towns or *burh*s that lie beneath many urban sites today.

As Christianity gradually re-established itself in Britain, a more sophisticated society emerged, with codified law and history, great centres of learning and glorious illuminated manuscripts. Religious sites – especially isolated ones such as Lindisfarne – became early targets of Viking raiders, who terrorized Britain's coastal regions from the end of the 8th century. Drawn by rich land and prosperity, they settled in towns and villages of the north and east. The defining conflict came against Norsemen in another guise: Duke William of Normandy's forces, who by their victory at Hastings changed the face of Britain for ever. The Conqueror's regime was harsh and repressive, yet it gave us the invaluable Domesday Book, a unique snapshot of life and how people actually lived it at the end of the first millennium.

PRECEDING PAGES: Inside the Farmer's House at West Stow Anglo-Saxon Village. The square 'fire box' in the centre, round shields, the wooden walls and floors all reflect archaeological evidence from the period. **DETAIL:** One of the Viking warriors who menaced the coasts of Britain throughout the 9th and 10th centuries.

BELOW: Norman women prepare for a marriage ceremony. After the Norman conquest, marriage was used to unite dynasties and consolidate land-holdings. **OPPOSITE:** A Romano-British warrior, poised to defend Pevensey Castle against the forces of the Saxon king Aella, who invaded in AD 491.

Visiting Saxon, Viking and Norman sites

RELATIVELY FEW BUILDINGS OR SITES survive from the period's early centuries, at least as recognizable structures – though their ghostly outlines may be seen in the landscape and within the shells of later constructions. Saxon stone churches such as Escomb in County Durham and St Paul's in Jarrow are still living parish churches, the focus of ordinary lives for hundreds of years. St Martin's in Canterbury is even older, probably of late Roman origin; the Kentish queen Bertha worshipped there before the arrival of St Augustine in AD 597. Many physical settings, from Sutton Hoo to Lindisfarne, Jorvik to Yeavering, are highly evocative – some complemented by ancient documents, others still being explored by archaeologists. And Norman castles and cathedrals continue to dominate the landscape, their presence and authority still powerful after almost 1000 years.

THE ANGLO-SAXON LANDSCAPE

Pevensey Castle neatly spans the period. Built towards the end of the 3rd century AD, it was one of the chain of forts known as the Saxon Shore, defending the coast against marauding Saxon pirates. Nearly 900 years later it also witnessed the landing of the invading Normans on 28 September 1066. William of Normandy is thought to have sheltered his troops there, using the protection of massive Roman walls and towers. Today these still stand to virtually their full height, their late-Roman D-shape probably designed as catapult mounts.

Saxon Shore forts were constructed all along the southeast coast, extending from Brancaster in Norfolk to Portchester in Hampshire. The fort of Richborough in Kent, built shortly after the Roman invasion in AD 43, was refortified as part of the chain, as was nearby Reculver, where there are also the ruins of one of Kent's earliest churches, part of a late 7th-century monastery. Although the urban life that the Romans had lived was alien to incoming Saxons, Angles and Jutes, they adapted and reused many Roman buildings in later centuries. Portchester became the fortified residence of a Saxon thegn, while a Norman keep and small oval huts, thought to have been monastic cells, were later built in Burgh Castle.

The first Saxon settlements were built of wood and consequently only a few have survived. West Stow in Suffolk is a valuable example of an entire Anglo-Saxon village, preserved virtually undisturbed under a thick layer of sand. Over 70 buildings were excavated and some have been reconstructed to find out how they were built, what

BELOW: Pevensey Castle in Sussex is still a formidable piece of military engineering, with much of its curtain wall still standing to almost full height. Strategically placed on the south coast, it is an evocative memorial to the troubled centuries between the Roman withdrawal and the Norman conquest.

ABOVE: An Anglo-Saxon interpreter feeds Rhode Island Red cross bantams at Bede's World. Although this is a 20th- century breed, the size of their bones reflects those excavated on 8th-century sites. Chickens, a source of eggs and feathers as well as meat, were important possessions for people reliant on their own livestock for sustenance.

'You drive several miles from home to get here, and then it hits you that, in the 8th century, people from a village like this would have hardly ever left it. Their whole lives would have been spent here, and the world outside must have been a frightening place.'

they looked like, and what they were used for. It was from the evidence found here that the traditional notion of the Saxons leading squalid lives in muddy holes in the ground was discarded. Many so-called 'pit' buildings are now thought to have been weaving sheds, with others used for storage. Those that may have been homes were floored over, providing reasonably large dwellings with a degree of comfort. On the West Stow site they were clustered round a slightly larger, rectangular hall, with two doors and a central hearth, which is where much of daily life would have gone on. Today West Stow is a fascinating place to visit, an experimental recreation of authentic Saxon life (page 75).

The Sutton Hoo escarpment, with its brooding, scrub-covered mounds, overlooks the inland tidal waters of the Deben estuary in Suffolk. It was probably the burial place of Raedwald, an East Anglian king who died around 625, and a magnificent ship burial was excavated there in the late 1930s. The splendid finds included a superb decorated helmet, a long sword with a jewelled hilt, silver bowls and spoons and a massive gold buckle with intricate carving, among many other objects celebrating the warrior king's status and providing for

ABOVE: This stone carving at Bede's World is based on an assembly of carved face and bronze stag found at the Sutton Hoo ship burial. The unusually naturalistic face, possibly from abroad, may have been part of a sceptre or other symbol of authority, or a pagan idol, intended to protect the warrior king in the afterlife.

'Never before has such terror appeared in Britain … nor was it thought that such an inroad … could be made. Behold the church of St Cuthbert, spattered with the blood of the priests of God, despoiled of all its ornaments; a place more venerable than all in Britain is given … to pagan peoples.'

ALCUIN, AFTER THE RAID ON LINDISFARNE IN 793

his needs in the afterlife. Nothing remained of the man himself: the acidity of the soil at Sutton Hoo destroyed even his bones and teeth. But a ghost of the ship in which he was buried, a symbol of vast power and wealth, was imprinted in the soil, in such detail that it has been possible to build a reconstruction. Only the mounds remain on the Sutton Hoo site today, but it is a powerful, disturbing place, used as a Saxon execution ground in later centuries.

No visible ruins of the Anglo-Saxon palace at Yeavering in Northumberland remain, but excavations have revealed that large rectangular halls once stood in a field below the Yeavering Bell hillfort. The atmospheric setting is thought to be that of a 7th-century royal villa once belonging to Edwin, king of the Northumbrians, and which the historian Bede called *ad Gefrin*. Bede records a grand, 36-day visit made by Edwin in 627, shortly after he had converted to Christianity, during which the queen's missionary bishop, Paulinus, baptized many of the locals in the River Glen. Artists' impressions of the great hall at the height of its splendour evoke the warrior feasts described in *Beowulf*, as well as the image cited by Bede, in which human life is compared to a sparrow fluttering out of the dark into the light and warmth of a noble's hall, and then returning to the dark again.

Offa, king of Mercia in the 8th century AD, built his famous dyke along the England/Wales border to prevent incursions by the Welsh. The dyke, longer than Hadrian's Wall and requiring the labour of thousands of men in its construction, originally ran for 240 km (150 miles) from Prestatyn to Chepstow. Natural features were used where possible and an earth embankment created along the rest of the line; it still reaches a height of 2.5 m (8¼ ft). Today the Offa's Dyke Path enables walkers to follow in the footsteps of the Saxons and Welsh, and imagine the dyke in its heyday of power and prestige.

WARRIORS FROM THE SEA

At the end of the 8th century, the first Viking raids on Britain's coasts heralded a new threat. Exposed monastic sites such as Lindisfarne, the site of a violent attack in 793, were particularly vulnerable. The *Anglo-Saxon Chronicle*, started at the court of Alfred the Great, records how Viking warriors killed many of the monks, desecrated the church and looted treasures and relics. They did not steal everything, however; the monks saved the famous Gospels and took St Cuthbert's body from the ravaged site to eventual sanctuary in Durham Cathedral.

Lindisfarne is remote enough today, accessible across its causeway only at low tide; how much bleaker and lonelier would it have been for the monks living there when the Vikings came. For over 200 years coastal communities must have lived in fear of these devastating raids. Danes mainly attacked the east coast of Britain, while Vikings from Norway raided on the west. Orboch on the Isle of Skye celebrates in its place-name the memory of the first settler there, a Norseman called Orri whose status as a second son drove him away from his birthplace to make his fortune elsewhere. The Clan MacLeod, the lairds of the island since the 13th century, still live in nearby Dunvegan Castle, and elsewhere on the island is a museum of clan history. The video telling the story is narrated in a deep, dark, spine-tingling voice that suspends reality and recreates those times of fear and uncertainty, of harshness and want, of menace coming at you from the sea.

The Vikings were not only raiders. They also settled in Britain, farming and trading with Scandinavia and sites on the east coast of Ireland. Some accepted Christianity, at least in part; many of the intricate crosses found in Britain – particularly in the Scandinavian-influenced north – combine Christian symbols with pagan carvings. Such 'documents' show the confusion and compromise of allegiances, political and religious, in those turbulent centuries.

ABOVE: A Viking warrior wearing an early type of Scandinavian helmet with spectacle-like eyeguards and mail neck protection. Bands of terrifying raiders attacked coastal regions, beginning with a ferocious assault on Lindisfarne, where many monks were killed and treasure looted.

RIGHT: Lindisfarne Priory on Holy Island is remote enough today, accessible across its causeway only at low tide; how much bleaker and lonelier it must have been to the monks who lived there when the Vikings came. Coastal communities were vulnerable to Viking raids for over 200 years, and it is easy to imagine the inhabitants' fear when visiting the desolate, wind-swept sites.

In the 9th century Viking settlement shaped the character of cities such as Jorvik (York). The living museum complex of Jorvik offers a close link between past and present in its display of the real excavation, including a (replica) skeleton in the actual grave where it was found, and 1000-year-old timbers still *in situ*. Even more realistic are faces in the display, created by scanning skulls of the period and superimposing the faces of modern people, many living in York today.

SECURING THE CONQUEST

The most enduring 'Viking' incursion was that of William of Normandy, a descendant of the Viking seafarer Rollo who came to northern France early in the 10th century. The site where William defeated the Saxon thegns at the battle of Hastings remains powerfully evocative: it is possible to imagine Saxon forces taking position at the top of Senlac Ridge and the Normans massing to attack from below. Re-enactors plot the fluctuations of the battle, culminating in the death of Harold – cut down by the swords of Norman nobles, but perhaps also with an arrow in his eye; the Bayeux Tapestry shows both. William built Battle Abbey on the site, with the church's high altar marking the spot where Harold fell. At first William refused Harold's body honourable burial, and it was shovelled into a makeshift grave; but it is likely that his remains were later reburied at Waltham Abbey.

Harder to bury were the rebellions of the Saxon population. It took several years for William to be secure on the throne, during which time he stamped his authority on the country with ferocious efficiency. The evidence of his conquest can be seen all over Britain, especially in the castles erected by the king and his nobles. Most were initially constructed in earth and wood, using the new motte and bailey design, but some, such as the famous White Tower, the core of the Tower of London, were always in stone. So was Richmond Castle in Yorkshire, one of the best preserved buildings of its age, with more 11th-century fabric than any other. A Norman curtain wall, uniquely well preserved, surrounds the castle's main enclosure for much of its length. Scolland's Hall in one angle of the castle is one of England's earliest domestic interiors. It brings the reality of castle existence – bleak and uncomfortable even for the wealthy – vividly to life.

Clifford's Tower in York, sitting on top of its high motte, is the most visible remnant of York Castle, first built by William in 1068 and massively refortified in stone during the reign of Henry III. York

ABOVE: Archers on horseback had an important role in Romano-British forces, but were used less by the Anglo-Saxons, who viewed bows and arrows mainly as a hunting weapon. Norman archers attacked Harold's *huscarls* with a penetrating rain of arrows at the battle of Hastings, shown on the Bayeux Tapestry; they also took part in Norman hunts.

OPPOSITE ABOVE: The regime of castle building instigated by William I was swift and efficient, though he also took advantage of existing fortifications such as those at Old Sarum. The Conqueror paid off his troops here once his throne was secure in 1070, and the area's first Norman cathedral was built on the site, later to be relocated to Salisbury.

OPPOSITE: One of the remarkable serendipities in Domesday Book is the discovery of entries for small places that have since become much larger and more important. This page for Warwickshire includes Birmingham – a very small and insignificant village.

Castle was attacked in 1069, when the local people allied with an invading Danish force – the Scandinavian Vikings were still at it – to overwhelm Norman garrisons. William's response was the 'harrying of the North', the laying waste of an entire region, which resulted in a massive death toll from famine and warned other would-be rebels that William was not to be antagonized. The brutality of this revenge is well documented by the Anglo-Norman monk Orderic Vitalis. Although an apologist for the Norman regime, Vitalis nonetheless condemned William roundly for the suffering and death he had inflicted: 'My narrative had occasion to praise William, but for this act, which condemned the innocent and guilty alike to die by slow starvation, I cannot commend him. I am so moved to pity that I would rather lament the griefs and suffering of the wretched people than make a vain attempt to flatter the perpetrator of such infamy.'

Among the greatest legacies of William the Conqueror's reign – and certainly the most remarkable – is Domesday Book, now held in the National Archives at Kew. This 'guidebook' to the lands held by the king and his subjects was compiled in unprecedented detail. Commissioned in 1085, two years before William's death, Domesday was the first attempt by a ruler of England to count and survey his entire kingdom. Work on it ceased in 1090, leaving some gaps in its coverage, but it still describes, in 900 pages and two million Latin words, more than 13,000 places in England and parts of Wales.

For a new ruling dynasty, Domesday was a useful tool for settling disputes about landholding, taxation and liability for military service. It also contains a wealth of information about England, its people and their ways of life, with valuable comparisons between the situation before 1066 and the date of compilation. The abbreviation TRE occurs throughout, for '*Tempore Regis Edouardi*' or 'in the time of King Edward', and figures are constantly given for 'then' and 'now'.

The rise and fall of particular sites in England can be traced from references to them in Domesday. Among the places mentioned is Dunwich, clearly a prosperous and thriving port on the Suffolk coast, but one already – as faithfully recorded in Domesday – losing land to the sea. The entry reads as follows: 'Edric of Laxfield held Dunwich in the time of King Edward as one manor; now Robert Malet holds it. Then 2 carucates of land, now one; the sea carried off the other. Always one plough in lordship. Then 12 bordars, now 2 and 24 Frenchmen with 40 acres of land, and they all pay all customary dues to this manor…. Then one church, now 3 and they pay £4 and 10 shillings. In total the value is £50 and 60,000 herrings as a gift. In the time of King Edward it paid £10.'

Dunwich continued to lose land and decline in importance. Today it is just a small village, still subject to coastal erosion. The Domesday Book that first recorded it still provides legally admissible evidence on title to land; it was cited in court as recently as 1960.

The Normans built many more castles, which can still be seen and visited. But they also carried out an energetic rebuilding programme on the sites of Saxon churches and cathedrals, one reason why few of the earlier buildings survived. The great Norman cathedrals include Peterborough, Ely, Norwich, Worcester and Durham – the most complete, unaltered example of Romanesque architecture in Europe, and a World Heritage Site. The majestic nave is 900 years old and looks much as it did when first built. Great stone piers, alternately huge single columns and clusters, support the nave vault, each incised with an individual geometric pattern. Dimly lit and dominating its surroundings from a raised peninsula, Durham Cathedral still conveys a sense of Norman power and permanence to a once rebellious region.

ABOVE: Durham Cathedral, now a World Heritage Site, became the burial place of St Cuthbert and the Venerable Bede. Both were placed in the Saxon precursor of today's Norman cathedral, and Cuthbert's shrine was well established by 995. Work began on the dominant new structure, a symbol of Norman power, in 1093, and continued until 1280.

'I unhesitatingly gave Durham my vote as the best cathedral on planet Earth.'

BILL BRYSON

Recreating the past

MANY OF THE MOST EVOCATIVE LIVING MUSEUMS from this period are on original sites, capturing the authentic flavour of everyday life and of the difference between various parts of the country. It was a time when people, for the most part, stayed where they were born for the whole of their lives, rarely venturing beyond their home territory and knowing and understanding very little of life elsewhere. Fashions, even for ordinary people, were distinctive and regional, reflecting religious beliefs and allegiances. The monk Alcuin upbraided the Northumbrians for continuing to dress like barbarians now that they were Christians, and it was sufficiently odd to be worthy of note that the daughter of the king of Thuringia, St Radegund, preferred her 'barbaric' costume even after becoming a Christian queen.

LIVING OFF THE LAND

Life in these centuries was mainly rural and frequently short, although a few survived to old age. Famine was a constant fear, often occurring, oddly, in July when barns were empty of the previous year's produce and the spring crops were not yet ready to harvest. Bede's World at Jarrow, where the 8th-century monk and writer lived, is a powerful

BELOW: A local lord and his servant pay a visit to the farming community of Bede's World. Horses were an important status symbol in the 8th century, when ordinary people seldom travelled far from their homes. Brightly coloured clothing, such as the lord's orange and red cloak, was also an indication of rank.

recreation of agricultural life on a historic site from about 1300 years ago. Ancient cereal and vegetable varieties are grown there on an experimental farm called Gyrwe (pronounced Yeerweh), the Old English name for Jarrow; they provide medicines as well as food and supply raw material for building work and crafts such as textile dyeing. Reeds and sedges were used in thatching, and coppiced hazel and willow produced flexible wands for building walls. Gyrwe includes breeds of sheep, pigs and oxen as close as possible to the period, all far smaller than modern breeds. Timber buildings draw on archaeological evidence to recreate as far as possible authentic structures of the time.

Bede's World offers real, hands-on experience of life in the Anglo-Saxon era. Interpreters in costume demonstrate a wide range of crafts: spinning, weaving, dyeing and embroidery; pottery-making with a hand-turned wheel; hurdle-making, bead-making, basket-making, forging and leatherwork. Preparations for feasts demonstrate cooking techniques and the Anglo-Saxon use of herbs and other ingredients. Some of the cerebral and artistic activities of the monastic community,

BELOW: Whole families participate in recreations of 5th–7th-century life at West Stow. Events on this authentic site include demonstrations of Anglo-Saxon crafts and technology, including weaving, cooking, metalwork and building techniques, but there is also time for feasts and storytelling around the communal hall.

such as calligraphy with quills, are also available. The presence of interpreters who make armour and demonstrate weaponry and combat brings home the precariousness of life at the time, and the constant threat of armed strangers riding menacingly into your village.

Another example of a recreated Anglo-Saxon farming village on an authentic site is West Stow, which, in the words of its original excavator, offers a 'living, experimental reconstruction of the past'. It is investigative archaeology in action, with each reconstruction testing different ideas and using as far as possible the tools and techniques available to those who really once lived here. Far from dry research, it offers direct and immediate experience of the past. Visitors can go into the houses, touch the furniture and feel the woven cloth, knowing that these things belong to this actual place.

West Stow is very much a working settlement, with looms in the weaving house and a forge in the workshop, used for demonstrations at special events. Living history interpreters of all ages also inhabit the site throughout August. Two or three extended families would have lived here when the settlement was at its peak, and it would have been pretty self-sufficient. The bones of pigs, cattle, sheep and goats were found on site, as well as dogs and cats. People ate fish, and among the remains of wheat, barley, oats and rye, a single pea was found. Today's farm grows these authentic crops and keeps chickens and pigs.

ABOVE: Gyrwe, the experimental farm at Bede's World, contains a number of authentic rare breeds. The Manx Loghtan ram is an ancient breed from the north of Britain. It normally has four horns, but this animal lost one when young.

Tablet weaving of decorative braids

1 To set up the loom, the warp threads have been passed through the holes in each tablet (small bone or wooden squares) and secured at each end.

2 For each row of weaving, turn all the tablets through a quarter- or half-turn. Pass the weft thread between the warp threads after each turn.

3 Vary the colours of the warp yarn and turn tablets in different directions to create intricate patterns on the braid, used to decorate belts, hems and cuffs.

Interpreters in costume bring West Stow's Anglo-Saxon village to life and demonstrate its culture and technology. Whole families dress in period clothes and join in cooking, games, chores and social activities. Authentic details of dress, jewellery and weapons often draw upon evidence discovered in graves, where the positioning of pins, brooches and belts indicates the style of dress. This occurs particularly in female graves from early Anglo-Saxon times, where brooches by the shoulders clearly fastened garments; but tools, shield bosses and spears replace them in male graves. Fabric is sometimes preserved in clasps, enabling re-enactors to reconstruct weave, pattern and colour.

The Viking city of Jorvik

Like West Stow, Jorvik, the recreation under Coppergate in York of the 10th-century Viking city, is on its actual site. A modern 'time capsule' carries visitors back to the teeming, prosperous, well-established community, recreated as it would have been at 5.30pm on 25 October 975. York at this time was turning into a metropolis with the technology for two-storey dwellings – hugely advanced for the time. Builders are seen digging out the cellars of houses in order to

strengthen them before putting the second storey on top, while other people are going about their daily business. Smells and sounds are everywhere: animals clucking and squealing, children chattering, a woman shouting in old Norse, a rumbling thunderstorm, the smell of wood smoke and gutting fish, and the heady scent of a meaty stew. There is also a quite disgusting cesspit, redolent of the fact that the overwhelming smell during these centuries in both towns and villages would have been of dung – human and animal.

A WORLD AT WAR

Re-enactments from this period often feature battles – appropriately for a world where conflict was a fact of life and boys of 12 swore oaths of allegiance. Re-enactors at Jorvik Viking Festival recreate battles at York, including hand-to-hand fighting, and and boats modelled on Viking longships row against each other on the river. A Viking long hall is peopled with re-enactors in costume who demonstrate how typical food was prepared, as well as weaving, carving and authentic crafts. Other Viking festivals may include a storm on a palisade, complete with central tower, drawbridge and gate, a fighting platform

OPPOSITE, ABOVE:
Seafaring Norsemen, from the Vikings to their later incarnation as Normans, were involved in battles across Europe. This well-padded warrior appeared in a recreation of the battle of Larissa in 1082, when Norman warriors clashed with Byzantine forces in northern Greece.

OPPOSITE, BELOW: Rowing races in reconstructed longboats are popular features of the Jorvik Viking Festival, held every February in York. Valiant crews, in authentic costume, have to contend with Yorkshire's winter weather, such as bone-chilling fog on the River Ouse.

ABOVE: Spectators in full costume enjoy the river races at the Jorvik Viking Festival, well buttoned – or rather brooched – up against the weather.

LEFT: Vikings and Saxons battle it out at the Jorvik Festival, demonstrating how massed spears were used in an attack. The spear was the main weapon for all ranks of warrior, and was often the first weapon to be used before the sword was drawn. At the start of a battle they were used as javelins, thrown from behind a shield wall as on the Bayeux Tapestry, but were later used as strong thrusting weapons when the enemy was in reach.

and a sally port – all revealing in impressive detail the tactical problems of attempting to scale a wall under fire. Some Viking recreations close with spectacular ship-burning ceremonies, in which ships are set alight by fire arrows or blazing torches thrown from a parade.

Re-enactments can never be totally realistic, because wounds and death are not an option, but they can be compelling and vivid experiences for participants and spectators alike. Authentic weapons and armour combine with the real sounds and smells of battle to bring it all as close as possible to what it would have been like. A group of Saxons and Romano-Britons at Richborough Castle really put their backs into the battle with deafening roars and screams, their clothes and armour torn and scarred from many such encounters. The finale of this re-enactment was a terrifying charge on the watching crowd, which made it all too easy to imagine how genuine Romano-British villagers must have felt when confronting a vicious hoard intent on real violence and destruction.

The use of a real historic site for a known historical event brings an extra drama and immediacy to the event. In AD 491 forces of the Saxon king Aella launched a ferocious attack on the Romano-British garrison defending Pevensey Castle, then known as Anderida. Violent skirmishes were recreated inside and outside the fort, with the most desperate struggle – for control of the gatehouse – taking place on a narrow bridge over the moat. Meticulously researched weapons and shields came into their own in the confusion of battle, and the sweat and dirt also looked very real on a hot summer day.

Aella's attack on the Saxon Shore fort was successful, and he became the first Saxon ruler to be recognized as 'Bretwalda' – ruler of Britain. His relatively early incursion was followed by many others,

ABOVE AND BELOW: Aella really did invade Pevensey, or Anderida, and slaughtered the Romano-British defenders in skirmishes outside the fort and on the bridge. Shields were made of wood with a central boss and an edge binding for strength.

'Aella beseiged Anderida and slew all the inhabitants, there was not even one Briton left there.'

THE ANGLO-SAXON CHRONICLE

and by AD 1000 England had become a melting pot of races: Celts and Britons, Anglo-Saxons, Jutes and Franks; Scandinavians whose ancestors had settled long ago, as well as more recent Viking incomers; even the southern kings were Danish for a while. This turbulent period is the principal focus of Regia Anglorum, a living history society which recreates both warfare and civilian, domestic activities. They have created two fictional settlements on their website, the village of Wichamstow and the manor of Drengham, and peopled both with named characters whose skills and activities reflect the demands of life at the time. Metalworkers and woodworkers were

Arming a Saxon warrior thegn

1 A wool or linen undershirt, gartered leggings and skullcap provide the underpinnings to the battledress.

2 A short-sleeved mail tunic goes over the undershirt. The shirt is well padded for additional protection.

3 A leather belt, worn over the mail coat, secures the sword – a warrior's most prized and valuable weapon.

4 A leather arm protector is buckled on to the right forearm. Armour for limbs was relatively rare in Saxon times.

5 An iron helm, possessed only by wealthier warriors, is placed over the head and tightly fitting skullcap.

6 The helmet, with protective cheek flaps and distinctive nasal guard, is secured with buckles under the chin.

7 A round shield, similar to those found in Saxon graves, and a finely honed axe complete the preparations.

8 The armed thegn waits for battle to begin. His unprotected legs were vulnerable, with amputations common.

important for a community dependent on making and maintaining its own weapons, while bakers, potters, blacksmiths and fishermen all played essential roles. Weavers and craftsmen working with bone and leather produced items of clothing: cloaks, tunics and dresses; buckles, pins, belts and the closed-in shoes which replaced Roman sandals. Historical background to both village and manor is researched in detail, and Regia Anglorum members recreate some of the conflicts that would have concerned Earl Godwin, whose fictional power base is at Drengham. The society participates in battles and races at the Jorvik Viking Festival; it owns and operates five full-scale ships, which are often rigged for sail to show the power of 9th-century technology.

Regia Anglorum's current major project is the construction of Wychurst, an 11th-century fortified manor house and related buildings near Canterbury. A sunken featured building, similar to those found on other Saxon sites such as West Stow, cottage and rampart around the site have already been built, but the centrepiece, a long hall (again drawing on buildings found at West Stow and

ABOVE: It was when hand-to-hand combat ensued, as in this re-enactment of the battle of Hastings on its original site, that axes, knives and swords came into their own. The heavy, two-handed axe was a fearsome weapon, but its disadvantage was that its wielder had to sling his shield across his back to leave both arms free and was therefore laid open to attack.

OPPOSITE: The main body armour of the Anglo-Saxon period was mail. It was made by cutting a thin strip of iron from a sheet, or winding iron wire round a cylindrical former before cutting it off and compressing the ends. Mail protected against the cutting edges of weapons and was usually worn over a thick, padded undershirt. known as a gambeson.

BELOW: Conical helms as shown on the left were the norm for all armies at this period, but the Normans also introduced full-face helmets with narrow eye-slits.

elsewhere) is still in progress. The intention is to create a living, working settlement, as close to reality as possible, although some aspects of life at the time may prove too much for 21st-century sensibilities. Rodents and insects would have infested the mud floors and roughly thatched roofs, and worms of varying kinds were the norm within the human digestive tract. Some of the most virulent ones had the disconcerting habit of suddenly emerging from one of the body's orifices – such as the corner of the eye socket!

People living in such conditions may have had more resistance to some forms of infection than ourselves, but armies of the 10th and 11th centuries were probably riddled with illness and disease. Wounds festered quickly under such circumstances and many died of injuries inflicted by a variety of weapons – spears, axes, broadheaded iron arrows and ferocious, single-edged knives called scramaseaxes. Swords were highly prized and often very ornate, with iron pommels and guards decorated with silver balancing the weight of the blade. They were slashing weapons with tapered blades, capable of causing severe damage; excavated skulls have been found where the bone has been sliced across from one side to the other.

Spears were the main weapon of Saxon and Norman conflicts, ranging from the light throwing spear or javelin to a thrusting spear with a lozenge-shaped head and a central ridge for strength. The Bayeux Tapestry shows spears being thrown overarm at the battle of Hastings, aimed at opponents' faces (especially the vulnerable eyes), throats and upper chests – too dangerous a technique for modern re-creations to use. Axes also feature prominently in the tapestry's battle scenes, especially the two-handed Dane-axe introduced by the Vikings in the late 10th century and swiftly adopted by Saxon forces. This was a fearsome weapon with thin section blades, designed to tear flesh apart, set on a sturdy ash haft up to 1.5 m (5 ft) in length.

Iron knives were used as everyday tools as well as weapons, but medium or larger scramaseaxes may well have served as swords for ordinary warriors. Langseaxes, clearly intended for fighting, had blades of 54–75 cm (22–30 in), ending in a lethal needle point. Thrust into the body, they would have had a similar effect to a penetrating spear. Shields and armour offered only limited protection – re-enactors have discovered that a hurled javelin can pass straight through a limewood shield and possibly into its owner. Mail, worn by Saxons as well as Normans, would have stopped the cutting edge of most weapons, but even when worn over padding did not prevent the body from being dangerously crushed by their impact.

By the 11th century mailshirts reached to the knees or just below, with sleeves to the elbow. They often had an integral hood covering the back and top of the head, neck and shoulders, while a 'ventail' section of mail folded up over the neck and chin. Long mailcoats were split at the groin, back and front, so that the wearer could ride a horse. Gambesons, probably made of woollen cloth plus layers of felt and leather, were worn under mailshirts; although none have survived, re-enactors confirm their necessity. Wealthier warriors were starting to wear mail chausses, or leggings – a wise precaution, as accounts of battles often mention men having their legs chopped off. Helmets varied in design from a domed style with cheek flaps to a conical helm; the nose guard protecting the face might be part of the frame or added separately. The best helmets were those hammered from a single piece of iron, and consequently stronger than riveted versions.

The daddy of all battle re-enactments of this era is the battle of Hastings. It is regularly recreated by military interpreters who form into the opposing armies on the very field where the battle was fought. This battle is unique in that it, and the events leading up to it, are

'We know a lot about the battle of Hastings from the Bayeux Tapestry, which is full of details about both armies and what happened. It is amazing that it was made at all, let alone that it survived, and from it we know much more about this distant battle than about some much more recent encounters.'

LEFT: Battle Abbey is the scene not only of regular recreations of the battle of Hastings but also of Norman jousts – activities that honed military skills throughout medieval times. The warrior on the right is actually having the best of it, with his lance aimed at his opponent's upper body and seemingly deflecting the other lance.

ABOVE: Norman cavalry at a re-enactment of the battle of Hastings. They played an important role later in the conflict, though the deep, cohesive Saxon shield wall limited their impact in the early stages. Cavalry, as here, were armed with spears that were hurled over the shield wall hoping to break the ranks. Despite their skill, the contest hung in the balance for much of the day.

recorded on the almost contemporary Bayeux Tapestry, which allows today's re-enactors to recreate details of design and colour as well as the ebb and flow of battle. The re-enacting armies look very alike in mailshirts and helmets of similar designs, as the real ones would have done, although Normans shaved the backs of their heads – a sensible response to wearing a helmet through long battles, let alone at other times – and Saxons had longer hair and Mexican-type moustaches. Both armies have kite-shaped shields, though some Saxons also had round ones. They made powerful defences: the shield ring formed by Harold's elite *huscarls* on Senlac Ridge was 10 men deep and virtually impenetrable. Norman cavalry, keeping shield-side to the Saxon 'wall', could only hurl spears into their ranks hoping to hit something, and for much of the day it was a very evenly matched struggle.

These centuries were times of change and turmoil about which there is still a great deal to learn. Well-informed re-enactments, practical experiments and living history recreations bring us closer to the people who lived then, challenging expectations and conventional opinion to illustrate the realities of those very distant lives.

The early medieval centuries saw a spate of castle building across England and Wales, as baronial factions challenged first Norman, then Angevin monarchs. From their regional power bases, local lords dominated their subjects' lives, demanding labour and

MEDIEVAL LIFE

taxes, enforcing feudal laws and calling men and boys to war. The Church also held great power, and generations of craftsmen worked on the magnificent abbeys and cathedrals that took centuries to build. Yet underlying society was the constant need to grow and harvest food, with years of plenty offset by famine, exacerbated in the 14th century by the devastating impact of the Black Death.

4

Approaching medieval times

THE MEDIEVAL CENTURIES are the stuff of historical romance, from legends of Robin Hood and an anachronistic King Arthur to highly charged tales of larger than life figures: Thomas Becket, the Princes in the Tower, 'bad' King John and 'good' King Richard, heroic warriors such as Henry V as portrayed by Laurence Olivier and Kenneth Branagh. It was a bloody period; the civil war of royal rivals Stephen and Matilda was followed by the Hundred Years War against France, continual battles with the Scots and the internecine Wars of the Roses – not to mention the Crusades in distant Palestine. Waging war was the main occupation of the ruling classes, as they sought to hang on to both lucrative French landholdings and English estates. When not actually fighting they were honing military skills in mock battles or tournaments, hunting and jousting, sporting the heraldic emblems that developed to identify armed knights during the Crusades. They celebrated the exploits of real and imaginary heroes

PRECEDING PAGES
MAIN PICTURE: The classic image of medieval combat. A Yorkist knight from the Wars of the Roses that dominated English aristocratic life in the 15th century.

DETAIL: A well dressed medieval lady wearing a fine lace wimple and elaborate jewellery.

– Charlemagne and Alexander, Troilus and Lancelot – in songs and chivalric poems at variance with the brutality of real medieval warfare.

Yet this world of great castles and battles, richly clad lords and ladies, was far removed from the relentless agricultural cycle driving most people's lives. Working the land without modern machinery or fertilizers was hard physical labour; a poor harvest spelt famine in winter and spring, and illness and early death were the lot of the common people. That most devastating of epidemics, the Black Death, hit the country like a hammer in the first half of the 14th century, killing half the population of London and at least a third of all English people. Writings of the period powerfully reveal the bewilderment of those who felt themselves abandoned by God and in urgent need of communicating their desolation and suffering to posterity. Latin graffiti scratched on the wall of the tower of Ashwell church in Hertfordshire, at a time when building had been abandoned for lack of labour, is eloquent: '*XLIX pestilencia*' – '(13)49 pestilence' followed by a later *cri de coeur* from people '*miseranda ferox violenta*', 'wretched, wild and driven to violence' witnessing 'a tempest on the earth' – '*in orbe tonat*'.

The belief that this was the punishment of God on a sinful people was the natural response in a world where Christianity lay at the heart of existence. Medieval abbeys and monasteries were economic powerhouses and centres of learning, and local churches had terrifying frescoes of the Last Judgement to ram home the message to a largely illiterate congregation. Meanwhile, great cathedrals dominated the cities and towns, hugely extravagant creations that took centuries to build and absorbed generations of individual lives.

This medieval perspective, combining sophisticated allegory with superstition and ignorance, is hard to reach; yet those who lived in these centuries have left their own words behind. The 15th-century Paston letters are first-hand evidence of a medieval marriage, full of high regard as well as mutual affection and trust. Sir John Paston, writing to his wife in about 1486, praises her skills as a herbalist and asks her to send her plaster of *Flos Unguentorum* to relieve an aching knee suffered by the king's attorney, as well as instructions for its application. In the *Canterbury Tales* Chaucer's brilliantly realized pilgrims reveal a whole panoply of 'modern' human preoccupations and foibles – vanity, greed, lechery and concern for social status – that bring these distant centuries much nearer to our own.

OPPOSITE: The infra-structure of medieval life is still to be seen in many of Britain's towns and cities. Lincoln is a famous example; its cathedral, seen here from Friar's Court, sits amidst a network of medieval cobbled streets and historic houses.

ABOVE: Battles from the Wars of the Roses are often re-enacted on their actual sites by troops in authentic armour and insignia, such as these Yorkist soldiers. The nobility and those in their service took the brunt of the slaughter in these violent conflicts, of little relevance to ordinary peoples' lives.

'... *so that the writing does not perish with the writer ... I leave parchment for continuing it in case anyone should be alive in the future.' An addition in a different hand then reads 'Here, it seems, the author died.'*

**AN IRISH FRANCISCAN MONK
DURING THE BLACK DEATH, 1348–50**

Visiting medieval sites

THE MAJOR MONUMENTS OF THE MIDDLE AGES are those of the two great edifices of state, the church and the nobility – cathedrals and castles, abbeys and great houses. Such powerful buildings have usually survived the centuries, even if in ruined or altered form. Many towns and cities also possess their twisting medieval street patterns, curving around historic marketplaces that once drove the local economy. In York, the Shambles – named for its origin as the street of the butchers – still has some of its medieval jettied timber buildings leaning out at first-floor level, sometimes so close to those opposite that you can (allegedly!) shake hands across the street. The famous galleried Rows of Chester, dating from at least the 14th century, are a unique English example of medieval two-tiered shopping, with shops at ground level and at first-floor level above (as well as sometimes in the crypts below).

The city of Lincoln has many reminders of its medieval past. Its magnificent cathedral is surrounded by medieval remains, some

RIGHT: Stokesay Castle in Shropshire is not a castle at all but a fortified 13th-century manor house, built by a rich Ludlow wool merchant. Its surviving fortifications show that ordinary – if wealthy – houses, as well as baronial castles, needed permanent defences in the turbulent Middle Ages.

LEFT: Warkworth Castle in Northumberland, strategically located on a bend in the River Coquet. It was a regional power base of the Percy family, prime movers in the volatile politics of the time.

BELOW: Jousts and single combats were important for keeping military skills sharp. Re-enactors demonstrate the flexibility of medieval armour, which allowed the wearer to move reasonably rapidly and (contary to myth) to mount and dismount a horse.

grand, such as the Bishops' Palace, others more domestic, like the extraordinary Jew's House on the appropriately named Steep Hill. The Jew's House, dating from 1170, is one of the oldest English houses still in use. It survived as it was built in stone, unusually for the time, and is a living memorial to Lincoln's important 12th-century Jewish community. Cobbled streets around the cathedral complement medieval building styles and materials, and the Norman High Bridge is England's oldest example of a bridge that has buildings on it.

CASTLES AND BATTLEFIELDS

Henry II was a great builder of castles, but he also enforced the 'licence to crenellate' introduced to control the anarchic flourishing of fortifications that occurred as Stephen and Matilda battled for the throne. Framlingham Castle in Suffolk was one of those destroyed on Henry's orders, to curtail the power of its owner, Hugh Bigod, already threatened by Henry's nearby castle at Orford. Castle building was a

costly business, and Orford is remarkable for its building records, which are the oldest in the country and still held at the National Archives in Kew; between 1165 and 1173, £1413 was spent on it – a huge sum in the days when the castle watchman's wages were one (old) penny a day – £1.52 a year in modern money. Despite the expense, medieval castles were designed for territorial domination, not for comfort. They were cold and draughty with rudimentary furniture, and they must also have been very smelly, from the ordure that would collect at the foot of the walls under the garderobes, and from the animals kept inside the walls. Later in the medieval period, however, when times were more peaceful, castles such as Bodiam in Sussex combined strength and protection with comfort and even elegance.

Borders were perilous places in medieval times – the need for defence is underlined not just by the great royal and baronial castles but also by the numerous smaller fortified houses found all along both the Welsh and Scottish borders. Aydon Castle, a manor house in Northumberland, was initially built without fortifications during an unusually peaceful interval in the 13th century, but had to have defences added when the normal situation resumed. In Shropshire, Stokesay Castle is one of the most splendid medieval fortified manor houses in the country. It was built by Lawrence of Ludlow, a wool

'My father was diligent to teach me to shoot, as other fathers were with their children. He taught me how to draw, how to lay my body to the bow, not to draw with the arms as other nations do, but with the strength of the body … '

HUGH LATIMER, BISHOP OF WORCESTER, MID-16TH CENTURY

The English longbow and its arrows

1 Warwick Castle's official archer displays his longbow and quiver of arrows at a medieval living history event. His bow, made from well-seasoned yew, is much taller than he is, and requires great strength to draw.

2 Arrows had to be fitted and loosed quickly in the heat of battle. An experienced longbowman reckoned to fire between 10 and 15 arrows a minute, and to have 6 arrows in the air at any one time – a devastating attack.

3 Fired with considerable force, arrows could wreak havoc – they were able to penetrate a mounted armed man's leg and wound his horse as well. Archers needed plentiful stocks of arrows, and their quivers were frequently replenished, sometimes by men whose dangerous task it was to run across the open land between the armies and retrieve spent arrows. However, archers were also expected to join in later stages of combat, hence the sword and small shield.

ABOVE: The ability to use the longbow effectively was vital for medieval men, and all boys were legally obliged to learn the skill from an early age. Many towns still have areas called The Butts which was where, every Sunday, young men gathered to practise. Archers' skeletons have been identified in battlefield grave pits by over-developed upper arm bones, caused by repeatedly drawing the bows. This phenomenon has also been found in re-enactors who use the traditional, heavy bows.

merchant, at the end of the 13th century, and is a successful combination of impressive fortification and family residence.

The landscape can also help in bringing medieval times to life. Recreations of great battles from the Wars of the Roses, such as Towton and Tewkesbury, use the authentic settings; the carnage was so great that the fields at both are still called Bloody Meadow. Towton was fought in atrocious conditions on Palm Sunday, 29 March 1461, between the armies of Yorkist Edward IV and Lancastrian Henry VI. It was a bitterly cold day, with heavy snow driven by strong winds, and unusually where both armies were skilled in the longbow's use, the archery duel proved devastatingly one-sided. Lord Fauconberg, the commander of the Yorkist archers, ordered his men to unleash one salvo only – at a time when the rate of fire could be between 10 and 15 arrows a minute – and then stand still. The enemy responded with the traditional ferocious 'storm of arrows', but the arrows fell far short in the snow and wind. The Yorkists had plenty of arrows left for their next salvoes, and could also collect up replenishments from those that had failed to reach their targets. They left some of these stuck upright in the ground to cause further mayhem during the later charge.

Towton was probably the bloodiest battle ever fought on British soil, compounded by the 'give no quarter' orders issued by Edward IV in revenge for the deaths of his father and brother at Wakefield four months earlier. The level ground at Towton offered no strategic advantage to either side and hand-to-hand hacking with pike and battle-axe continued all day. When the late arrival of reinforcements under the Duke of Norfolk further weighted the balance in the Yorkists' favour, the rout that followed killed thousands. Many were drowned or hacked to death as they tried to cross the fast-flowing River Cock, said to be choked with bodies and running red with blood. The battlefield is today still broadly as it was in 1461 and the Towton Battlefield Society hold regular walks over the site, including a memorial walk every year on Palm Sunday.

It was not just the nobility who were massacred. At Towton a recently excavated grave pit revealed the remains of several men who had probably been captured in the rout after the battle and mutilated before being killed: their arms appeared to have been tied behind them and chopping marks on their skulls indicated that their ears and noses may have been cut off. These men were probably archers, for whom the worst excesses of retaliation were usually reserved.

The power of the church

The church in medieval times was not just one of the central pillars of power; it lay at the centre of the economy, with its vast landholdings and huge wealth. Much of this wealth was to be found in monasteries. Yorkshire alone could boast dozens of the magnificent religious houses that dominated local communities, crowned perhaps by Fountains Abbey, now a World Heritage Site. Rievaulx Abbey, even in its ruined state, still towers over the little village that surrounds it in its valley, while the remains of the huge circular window in the west front of the church at nearby Byland Abbey are vivid evidence of the effort and resources put into these remote buildings. To visit Mount Grace Priory on a snowy winter's day, with the paw marks of rabbits pocking the velvety white landscape, is to come a little closer to the isolation and peace of the Carthusian monk's life. Each had his own private, solitary cell with a little garden and outdoor lavatory – very civilized for medieval times, and a lot better than the smoky hovels of the rural poor. A monk's cell has been recreated at Mount Grace, pointing to

ABOVE: Gloucester Abbey is noted for its splendid south window, beautiful cloisters and a magnificent Perpendicular choir – all products of the medieval age. Its status and prosperity were greatly enhanced by pilgrimages to the tomb of Edward II, murdered in nearby Berkeley Castle but never officially canonized. Gloucester Abbey became a cathedral after Henry VIII's dissolution of the monasteries, and it remains one of the finest in England.

'We make medieval timepieces to show how the hours were measured … not everyone knows now that in the Middle Ages every day was divided into twelve hours of daylight and twelve of darkness, and the length of the hours varied according to the time of year.'

BELOW: A Cistercian monk at Cleeve Abbey with the wife of one of the abbey's rich benefactors. Endowments were rewarded with regular prayers for the donor and his family, showing the importance of the church in daily medieval life. Some monks were teachers, others highly skilled in medicinal remedies, several of which are still used today.

the discipline and dedication required to maintain this life of prayer, meditation and solitude – all for the greater glory of God.

There are ruins of abbeys and priories all over the country, in various states of preservation. At Wenlock Priory the 12th-century lavatorium – a Norman communal washbasin – survives pretty much intact, while Cleeve Abbey is one of the few 13th-century monastic sites where there is a full set of cloister buildings, together with a floor of medieval tiles and 15th-century wall paintings.

It is the great cathedrals still in daily use – Lincoln, Salisbury, Durham, Canterbury, York Minster, Gloucester, Wells, to name only a few – that bring us closer than almost anywhere else to the medieval mind. The grandeur of their conception and magnificence of the construction must have been overwhelming in comparison with the low-level settlements around them. Locations were chosen with care: Durham and Lincoln on their hills, Salisbury with its highest-of-all spire, Ely with its splendid octagon crowning the building and visible for miles over the Fens around…. Glorious details, from delicate tracery in vaults and windows to the exuberant foliage decorating the pillars of Southwell Minster reveal the skill and devotion of generations of masons and craftsmen. They often left their signatures in small carvings on misericords and roof bosses, some hardly visible to the naked eye but full of vivid detail, individual faces and dramatic action. A scowling wife beats her cowed-looking husband on a misericord at Carlisle Cathedral, while a gargoyle in Lincoln Cathedral has become known as the mischievous Lincoln Imp.

A fine 14th-century roof boss in Exeter Cathedral shows the murder of Thomas Becket. The small spherical carving finds room for Becket himself, the four murderous knights and the clerk trying to stop the killing; all their armour, clothing, hairstyles and facial expressions are carefully sculpted. Canterbury became the greatest centre of medieval pilgrimage after Becket's murder, to the fame and enrichment of the cathedral and its city. The steps leading up to the Trinity Chapel in the cathedral have been worn smooth from countless pilgrims' feet down the centuries. It is easy to imagine the scenes in the narrow medieval streets, still thronged with visitors coming to pay their respects, though more likely now as tourists. Pilgrimages do continue today, however, expressions of a living faith that has lasted through the centuries. The shrine of Our Lady of Walsingham in Norfolk is still a pilgrimage site, as is Glastonbury, with its mysterious associations with St Patrick, King Arthur, Joseph of Arimathea and the Holy Grail. The George and Pilgrims Inn at Glastonbury is a fine example of a pilgrims' inn, developed from the monastery guest house and erected in its present form in 1475.

THE MEDIEVAL COUNTRYSIDE

The medieval economy was a rural one, and the traditional system of strip farming – the 'open field' system – has left its mark all over the country. Gentle undulations of ridge and furrow, with their distinctive 'reversed-S' curve, are the legacy of medieval villagers who trudged along the strip behind an ox-drawn plough. They occur particularly in the Midlands, most dramatically in Laxton in Nottinghamshire – a village that through one of the accidents of history never replaced the medieval system with the practice of enclosure. Here, three open fields still cover 194 ha (480 acres), and 14 open-field farmers are allotted their own strips within them.

Another visible relic of medieval life is the 'deserted village', often abandoned after plague killed the local labour force. Hundreds of them exist, mostly clustered in a broad band running from the north-east of England to the southwest, with an outlying group in Norfolk.

BELOW: The Domesday entry for Wharram Percy in Yorkshire shows a thriving small village which, like all such places, had its own church. Now deserted, its church ruins are surrounded by humps and hollows – the small houses and gardens of the medieval settlement.

LEFT: Hendre'r-ywydd Uchaf farmhouse, from Llangynhafal, Denbighshire, rebuilt at the Museum of Welsh Life. This single-storey building is typical of a good quality Welsh farmhouse in medieval times. Its roof and walls are supported on four sets of oak 'crucks', dividing the building into five sections or bays: the lower two for cattle and the upper three for the family. Outside walls are timber-framed, made of panels infilled with wattle and daubed with clay covered in limewash.

Recreating the past

RE-ENACTMENTS OF THE MEDIEVAL PERIOD often focus on the military, reflecting the fascination of great battle set-pieces and the weaponry used by those who took part in them. But there is a great deal more to recreate, from fairs and festivities to traditional sports and jousts, all drawing on the music, foods, practical crafts and costumes that bring the period to life. Many medieval buildings are still used for their original purpose, providing evocative settings for living history events. Living museums across the country have rescued thousands more structures from oblivion and reconstructed them to give an authentic flavour of life as it was experienced so many centuries ago.

'Many people think that the most difficult thing about medieval cooking is using the open fire. But for me, the strangest thing is the lack of forks; you just have to hang on to your knives.'

RIGHT: A young woman prepares home-grown food in the medieval crofter's cottage at Ryedale Folk Museum. This typical village dwelling of the 13th–16th centuries, without internal partitions, would have housed family and livestock. Food was seasonal, regional and organic, but supplies could be precarious. Crops were vulnerable to the weather, to pests and to marauders, all of which might bring famine to otherwise self-sufficient communities.

The Weald and Downland Museum in Sussex has a wealth of such buildings, including a medieval shop that once stood in Middle Street, Horsham. When it was dismantled the timbers were found to be heavily sooted, indicating open fires burning over a long period, perhaps for the production of food items for sale. Medieval shops usually took the form still to be seen in some fishmongers, with an open front and a counter to display goods. Another reconstruction, Bayleaf Farmstead, dates mainly from the early 15th century; although not large, its high, open hall conveys a sense of grandeur. The upper chamber, known as the solar, was the family's private bed-sitting room and has its own garderobe. Weald and Downland also has one of the few examples of an early aisled hall to survive intact, and a thatched, flint-built cottage from a deserted medieval village near Brighton – probably built in the 13th century and abandoned in the early 15th.

The Museum of Welsh Life also features a number of medieval buildings re-erected in its grounds. One of these is Hendre'r-ywydd Uchaf farmhouse, originally from Denbighshire (page 94); dating from 1508, it is typical of higher quality Welsh medieval farmhouses.

MEDIEVAL LEISURE

The people of the medieval centuries can be powerfully brought to life through recreations using places where they lived or visited. A royal progress recently staged at Carlisle Castle brought Edward I back to a familiar haunt – his campaign base in wars against the Scots, where he held several parliaments, and close to where he died in 1307. The king, in his new incarnation, looked tall and regal (his nickname was Longshanks as he towered over his subjects), with long curly hair. His queen, Eleanor, wore a wimple over her hair, and a long flowing dress. Their robes, fastened by a shoulder brooch in those days before buttons, looked comfortable and functional rather than extravagant, but the rich material and quality of workmanship proclaimed their worth. The royal couple sat on thrones to be entertained by a troupe of players, performing at the expense of their host, the castle warden. Before them were earthenware jugs and silver dishes from which the king selected delicacies such as apricots on the point of his knife – forks were not used – for himself and Eleanor. He rewarded the actors with a piece of fruit each, proffered on the point of his own knife.

The clothes, stories, dishes and food are all extensively researched and contemporary with Edward's time, although the court would have

ABOVE: Arrows had different types of head for a variety of purposes, all designed to inflict the maximum damage; imagine trying to pull the one on the left out of a flesh wound! Their lethal nature was enhanced by the archers' habit of sticking them point down in the ground before firing, adding dirt and the possibility of infection to the hazards they would inflict.

OPPOSITE: All facets of medieval life, costumes and activities are open to present-day interpreters. Thorough research and careful preparation informs their roles, the source of much enjoyment to participant and spectator alike.

spoken medieval French. A lutenist played music of the time, on a recreated medieval lute. Musical instruments are researched, made and played, often in costume, by societies such as Musica Antiqua. Some are familiar to modern ears, such as the harp and bagpipes; others less often heard are the shawm, crumhorn, rebec and dulcimer.

Travelling actors, such as those in the recreation at Carlisle, often played at medieval courts. Other leisure pursuits for the nobility kept combat skills sharp: hunting and hawking, jousting, mock battles and tournaments. Jousting was a courtly pursuit, often undertaken in honour of a knight's lady, but its warlike origins were never far from the surface and it could be dangerous. Modern jousts are very popular, and genuinely competitive; they also demand great care and skill from their participants. The lances have breakaway wooden ends, and the aim is to break your lance against your opponent, winning a whole point if the lance breaks cleanly or half a point if it is a glancing blow, called an attaint. If the re-enactment is of a 14th-century joust, the knights wear some body armour and carry shields; later in the 15th

BELOW: Re-enacted jousts are hugely popular events, not least because of the colourfully dressed, specially trained horses. They can reach speeds of up to 25mph, even when carrying a knight in full armour that weighs around 3.2 kg (5 stone).

ABOVE LEFT AND TOP:
The matching livery of both
knights and horses in jousts
ensures maximum
recognition from the crowd.
In medieval times livery was
essential for identification,
since there were no uniforms
and knights increasingly wore
closed-face helmets (such as
the pig-faced bassinet, above
left). The drama is enhanced
by the fact that these tough
events are played for real; the
attrition rate at jousts is high,
despite lances that fracture
easily, and combatants are
not infrequently injured.

century there were no shields and full body armour was worn, so that
the lances would break against the body or the head. Modern
armourers need hundreds of man-hours to make this armour, which
consequently costs up to £12,000. However, it is flexible and relatively
light-weight, and people – even modern ones, not used to wearing it
– can move quite easily, and even roll around and do handstands.

Horses can be more of a problem; few will willingly charge
against another horse, particularly when it is wearing a colourful,
flapping caparison topped by a ferocious-looking rider. Specialist
stables train and hire out horses for jousting, but they are rare creatures
– as was the case in the past, too. Letters exist from the late 15th
century in which the Duke of Burgundy, the richest man in Europe,
asks the King of England for a loan of certain named horses for a joust.

MEDIEVAL COMBAT

High-quality re-enactors know the history of their periods intimately
and are very specific about their activities. Medieval military specialists
pay great attention to the detail of armour and weapons, as well as the
strategies and fluctuations of the military actions that they recreate.
It is a Victorian myth that those wearing medieval armour had to be

winched into their saddles; in reality, soldiers dismounted and fought on foot, as Edward IV did at Towton, and armour had to be light and flexible enough to allow its wearer to run, fight and get up after a fall. Medieval warriors were used to armour, but its effect after hours of battle would have been utter exhaustion – a severe impediment for a knight trying to flee the field. And the joints and chinks necessary for armour's flexibility offered – particularly when it was getting old and worn – ample openings for lethal arrows.

The most popular helmet during the Wars of the Roses was the sallet. This covered the whole head, sweeping away at the back to

'All women had to know how to armour a knight in the Middle Ages, since they could be called upon to do it at any time. I sometimes dress as the knight's wife and sometimes as a maidservant – both are equally authentic.'

Arming Sir Thomas Erpyngham

1 The padded acquiton (undershirt) is followed by leg harness – cuisse, poleyn (at the knee) and greaves.

2 The arm harness is attached to the mail shirt with leather thongs. Suspenders hold leg armour in place.

3 A mail collar, or pigsain, protects neck and shoulders, and covers the shoulder attachment points.

4 The bassinet is placed over a linen arming cap. A mail aventail is attached to the vervaise at its edge.

5 After the surcoat decorated with his arms and insignia, the great helm is added. In Sir Thomas's case, this is topped with an imposing ducal coronet. Arming was always done from feet upwards, and the ensemble weighs about 51 kg (112 lb).

protect the neck and with only a slit at the front through which to see. It gave good protection – but the blinkered vision must have increased discomfort hugely during a long and bloody conflict. Medieval battle was in fact supremely uncomfortable. Armour chafed and the wearer became drenched with sweat whatever the weather; shoulders and arms grew bone-weary from the weight of weapons and the relentless heave and thrust of using them; ears were assailed by the roars and screams all around, compounding the adrenalin-fuelled fear; and ground underfoot quickly became slippery with blood and clogged with bodies. Horses could trample on those on foot, and friends could be lethal in the event of a panic-stricken stampede. Dehydration was a great problem, and those in full armour had to take frequent breaks for a drink – exposing themselves to sniper bowmen.

Victories at Crécy in 1346 and Agincourt in 1415 were achieved through the supremacy of the English longbow, which mowed down the front French ranks with devastating effect. The famous 'storm of arrows' is recreated by today's re-enactors (at the Weald and Downland Museum, for example), showing what it must have been like to see that dark cloud of death approaching. The rate of fire was very fast – skilled bowmen reckoned to have six arrows in the air at once – and opposing levies could only stand and endure. Seasoned veterans knew to keep their helmeted heads well down – a curious glance skyward could all too easily result in blindness or death.

The English longbow was so successful that the few crossbowmen in medieval campaigns were mostly European mercenaries – like the one who fatally wounded Richard I at a castle he was besieging near Limoges. A crossbowman in the Medieval Siege Society owns his own recreated 15th-century crossbow. He uses bolts with sharp tips (called piles) for practice and demonstration, but is issued with rubber-tipped bolts for recreated battles. His armour is meticulously researched. It includes a full breastplate and a visored sallet, plus arm and leg harness, with cuisses over his thighs. Underneath he wears a padded arming jack complete with sewn-in mail panels, to protect danger areas such as the armpits. Under the jack are linen underpants and woollen hose with a built-in codpiece. Mail trunks or a short mail skirt gave more protection for that vulnerable area.

Some societies focus on individual battles, such as the Tewkesbury and Towton Battlefield Societies, while others, for

'An arrow pinned the thigh of a soldier to his saddle, although the skirt of his leather tunic was there to protect him outside and inside the leg. He tugged on the reins and pulled his horse round in a half-circle, whereupon another arrow, shot by the same bowman, hit him in exactly the same place in the other thigh, so that he was skewered to his horse on both sides.'

THE LATE 12TH-CENTURY TRAVELLER AND WRITER GERALD OF WALES (GIRALDUS CAMBRENSIS), ON THE SKILLS IN ARCHERY OF THE MEN OF SOUTH WALES

The crossbow

1 A crossbow archer 'spans the bow' by hand, one foot resting in the stirrup. The bowstring is pulled up to a notched nut which holds it taut. Crossbows were made from hardwoods such as oak and beech.

2 The crossbow bolt is loaded on to the bow. A bolt has a wooden shaft with a forged and tempered iron tip, and flights made of feathers, parchment or leather. Flights are attached to the shaft with hemp.

3 The crossbowman shoulders his unloaded bow; it was a formidable weapon despite its small size and relatively light weight (about 1.8– 2.3 kg or 4–5lb). Draw weights were significant (about 40–50 kg/ 90–110 lbs).

example the Medieval Siege Society, are more general. They explore life in a campaign camp, using authentic armour and weapons, cooking and eating period food. Recreations include set-piece battles and medieval fairs, such as the one at Herstmonceux Castle in Sussex, where combat and archery displays take place alongside jousts, falconry, fire-eaters and craft stalls.

DOMESTIC LIFE

The tentacles of the Black Death in the 14th century reached everywhere, and its effects changed the country irrevocably – much more so than the constant wars that had less impact on everyday lives. Unless you lost one of your menfolk in a battle, or were unlucky enough to be in the way of the armies, life for most people went on much as normal – with shortages, famine and unrelenting hard work.

Bread was the staple food, baked at home or by professional bakers in towns. Brown bread also had a function as the trencher, or plate, on which other food was served. Large, four-day-old loaves were cut into thick slices and piled with food, eaten with knives and spoons; two people usually shared a portion or 'messe'. Fish was an important food, not just for its nutritional value, but also because the medieval church laid down rules for meat-eating: it was forbidden for about half the year at the height of the medieval period. The legacy of 'fish on Friday' (that is, abstinence from meat) was a rule within the Catholic church until the mid-20th century, and is still a convention.

Gardens were vital adjuncts to rural cottages, where vegetables were grown along with a wide range of herbs used in cooking and as medicine. The crofter's cottage garden at the Ryedale Folk Museum has beds of peas, beans, leeks and onions, as well as colewort (an early cabbage) and the now rare Good King Henry, or fat hen. Herbs grown there include comfrey for fractures, feverfew for migraine and wormwood for intestinal worms, as well as mugwort to fend off evil spirits. The museum also grows old varieties of fruit local to the area, such as Coes golden drop plum and the Alexander apple.

The medieval centuries are a bewildering mixture. They were a time of poverty and hardship, ignorance and superstition, but they also saw the creation of magnificent buildings and works of art, using only simple tools and technology. Their great legacy of architecture, writings and paintings gives plenty of clues for today's re-enactors as they recreate the lives of those who inhabited this fascinating period.

ABOVE: Authentic cooking techniques, such as sautéing simple oatcakes on a dry griddle, allows re-enactors and spectators to get a real sense of medieval food. It also brings home to cooks the labour involved in doing everything from scratch.

BELOW: These medieval winklepickers indicate that fashion has always been with us when it can prevail over practicality. It was for the rich, however; those lower down the social scale either made their own shoes or went barefoot.

THE GREAT CHANGES OF THE TUDOR AND STUART

CENTURIES AFFECTED PEOPLE FROM EVERY WALK OF

LIFE. HENRY VIII INSTIGATED THE REFORMATION,

A HAMMER BLOW THAT DESTROYED ENGLAND'S

MEDIEVAL RELIGIOUS FABRIC, FLATTENING MANY OF

ITS INSTITUTIONS. YEARS OF RELIGIOUS TURMOIL

TUDORS, STUARTS & THE CIVIL WAR

WERE THE RESULT, YET HIS REIGN, AND THAT OF HIS

DAUGHTER ELIZABETH, SAW A FLOWERING OF THE

ARTS AND A BURGEONING NATIONAL IDENTITY.

JAMES I'S UNION OF THE ENGLISH AND SCOTTISH

CROWNS OFFERED A PROSPECT OF PEACE, BUT LATER

IN THE CENTURY A BRUTAL CIVIL WAR DIVIDED

FAMILIES AND RUINED FRIENDSHIPS. PARLIAMENT'S

EVENTUAL VICTORY LED TO CHARLES I'S EXECUTION

AND A DECADE OF COMMONWEALTH RULE.

5

Approaching Tudor and Stuart times

THE TUDORS ARE THE MONARCHS whom perhaps we now feel we know best – mainly because they were such larger than life characters. The Stuarts, with the exception of the 'Merrie Monarch' Charles II, may have been less glamorous, but they were still vivid personalities, and their era is the stuff of popular legend as well as novels and films.

The dramatic incidents of their reigns are well known: Henry VIII's break with the Roman Catholic church and the dissolution of the monasteries that followed; the defeat of the Spanish Armada under Elizabeth and the flowering of an Englishness celebrated in plays and poems, magnificent buildings at home and daring exploration abroad. The Stuarts united Scotland and England under one crown but their reigns remained troubled: the Gunpowder Plot and the Civil War; the Commonwealth and the Restoration; the devastating plague followed by the Great Fire of London, with diarists such as Samuel Pepys offering fascinating perspectives into the realities of everyday life.

It was a volatile age in which shifting political fortunes could all too easily send the great and good from palace to prison, often through the dreaded Traitor's Gate at the Tower of London, where Anne Boleyn fell to her knees in terror and her daughter, Elizabeth, fearing that her half-sister, Mary, would order her execution, refused to get out of the boat. The Tower had huge symbolic importance as a prison-fortress in those perilous times of religious persecutions, conspiracies and the waxing and waning of political influence. The execution block on Tower Green, inside the walls, was reserved for the privileged few – such as Anne Boleyn and Catherine Howard, Lady Jane Grey and the Earl of Essex – while the scaffold on Tower Hill, where huge crowds could watch, was the site of most executions. London Bridge was one place where heads were displayed, and the city gates still bore the heads of those who signed Charles I's death warrant seven years after execution – the last vengeance of his son.

Even ordinary people in those centuries could become entangled in the great affairs of state. The massive upheaval of the Reformation struck at the bedrock of religious faith and affected everyone at a personal and immediate level. Fires of religious turmoil caught up ordinary people such as Joan Waist of Derby, a poor blind woman who had saved up for a copy of the English New Testament and paid people to read it to her. The Civil War also divided families and inflicted the horrors of war indiscriminately as cities and towns were besieged and battles and skirmishes took place all over the country.

Visiting Tudor and Stuart sites

THESE WERE CENTURIES of unprecedented destruction, as the medieval abbeys and monasteries were plundered for stone or allowed to fall into ruin, and castles and great houses were wrecked by sieges in the Civil War. Yet the confidence and prosperity of the age also led to some of Britain's most magnificent architecture. The glorious London churches of Hawksmoor and Wren, crowned by the splendour of St Paul's Cathedral, replaced those of the medieval city, destroyed in the Great Fire. Elaborate palaces, from Hampton Court to Blenheim, combined with new military fortifications and expanding dockyards to reflect the hopes and fears of those turbulent, expansionist times.

DEFENDING THE REALM

The early 16th century saw recurring conflict against the Scots, French and Spanish. Henry VIII's invasion of France, early in his reign, caused the French to invoke the 'auld alliance' with the Scots, who invaded Northumberland. Scottish forces under James IV captured both the small, picturesque castle at Etal and the mighty fortress at Norham, towering over the River Tweed; but a few weeks later they suffered devastating defeat by Henry's northern levies at the battle of Flodden.

ABOVE: A Tudor cannon in action. The early 16th century saw the beginnings of artillery, still unreliable but an increasingly formidable weapon. The invading forces of Scotland's James IV used heavy cannon to great effect on Norham Castle, which needed considerable rebuilding as a result.

RIGHT: St Mawes Castle, built by Henry VIII in the early 1540s, faces its larger neighbour, Pendennis Castle, across the Fal estuary. St Mawes both illustrates Tudor technological prowess and celebrates the power of the monarch, and is still impressively complete.

Later in his reign, Henry VIII's repudiation of papal power made him the enemy of Catholic Europe, and he instituted a new round of defence and castle building. Of the three ' Henrician castles' along the east Kent coast, Deal and Walmer have survived. The latter has been converted into a comfortable home, but Deal Castle retains a military feel. It is not at all ruined, but it is empty, and the passages under its perimeter walls are dark, echoing and often flooded. Deal is a chilly place, and the 'murder holes' in the gateway's ceiling are a grim reminder of the castle's origin in an ever-present threat from the sea.

The string of new forts around the south coast culminated in the twin castles of Pendennis and St Mawes, which face each other across the Fal estuary. Both castles were active in the Civil War and in World War II, when they were almost 400 years old – testimony to the skill of their builders and engineers; details of gun loops, windows and carvings also reveal impressive care, St Mawes remains much as it was when it was built, reflecting the lives of the ordinary soldiers in its garrison and of those who mustered there in times of danger.

Whereas the Tudors built and maintained castles and defences, the Civil War witnessed the 'slighting' or destruction of fortifications to prevent their use by the other side. At Helmsley Castle in Yorkshire, huge sections of the east tower still lie in the ditch where they fell when blown up after the Royalist garrison was starved out in 1644. Beeston Castle was partly destroyed in the same way, but Pendennis and St Mawes were spared because of their strategic value.

ABOVE: Landsknechts, German mercenaries employed by several Tudor monarchs, in parade at Kirby Hall. Famous for garish costumes, they were a formidable force, using pikes 6.5m (18 ft) in height as well as huge, two-handed swords.

BELOW: The gatehouse of Carisbrooke Castle on the Isle of Wight. This early 12th-century castle became Charles I's prison for much of 1648 after he escaped from Hampton Court and turned himself in to Col. Hammond, the Governor of Carisbrooke.

RIGHT: The *Mary Rose*, at the Historic Dockyard in Portsmouth, is the world's only 16th-century warship. The ship's framework is displayed, together with remarkably preserved artefacts that show how sailors lived on board. Recovered remains of sailors show them to have been young, fit men with an average height of 1.7m (5 ft 7 in) whose surprisingly nutritious diet included salted meat, fish and fresh fruit.

ABOVE: A 64-pounder cannon at Upnor Castle in the Thames estuary. The Tudor fort, built to protect naval dockyards at Chatham, reveals at low tide stumps of a pointed timber palisade of 1599, designed to defend the angled water bastion.

Carisbrooke Castle on the Isle of Wight served as Charles I's prison after his surrender to the island's Parliamentarian governor, Colonel Hammond. The king tried twice to escape; on the first occasion he got stuck in the bars of the window, and on the second he was foiled by Hammond, who arrived in the room with the words 'I am come to take leave of Your Majesty, for I hear you are going away.' The windows – and bars – of Charles' bedchambers can still be seen, though one of them was replaced in 1856.

The royal dockyards of Portsmouth, Woolwich, Deptford and Chatham were all established by Tudor monarchs, who recognized the importance of a strong navy for an island nation. Little remains of the original dockyards, adapted for new technology through the centuries, although a few of Portsmouth's historic gates survived World War II bombing and the Commissioner's House at Chatham, with its painted ceiling, dates from 1704. An Elizabethan artillery fortress at Upnor was designed to protect Chatham's dockyards as well as warships anchored in the river, although it could not prevent the Dutch fleet causing severe damage in the Second Dutch War of 1667.

The most dramatic evocation of naval life in Tudor times was raised from the seabed 20 years ago. The *Mary Rose*, Henry VIII's favourite warship, keeled over and sank near Portsmouth in 1545 *en route* to battle with the French. It is a fascinating time capsule of Tudor life, containing cannon, longbows and arrows, gold coins, items of silk clothing, musical instruments, tankards, food and gaming boards.

BELOW: John Smithson, architect of the Little Castle at Bolsover (behind), during a recreation of Charles I's visit there in 1634. He holds plans of the castle, whose development he took over from his father, Robert Smythson, changing his surname's spelling in the process. The doorway and balcony were influenced by details of some of Inigo Jones's London buildings; inside, the house is full of allegorical images, centred on the battle of good and evil.

RIGHT AND OPPOSITE: Audley End House in Essex, originally three times as large as today, is one of the finest Jacobean houses in England. It has been much altered over the centuries, but the Grand Hall retains its magnificent Jacobean screen and ceiling, and the River Cam still flows through the grounds. Described by James I as 'too big for a king, but would do well for a Lord Treasurer', it reflects the prosperity and confident expansion of the 16th and 17th centuries.

GREAT TUDOR AND STUART HOUSES

Many great builders flourished in the Tudor and Stuart period, such as Bess of Hardwick; Chatsworth was her main home, but she also built a magnificent house at Hardwick in Derbyshire. Bolsover Castle, also in Derbyshire and built by the Cavendish family in the 17th century, offers magnificent views over surrounding countryside from its high bluff. Although many parts are now ruined, the Little Castle at Bolsover is still much as it was when built for leisure and enjoyment. It features magnificent hooded fireplaces of alabaster and marble, and allegorical wall paintings full of fashionable symbolism.

Probably the grandest surviving royal palace of both the Tudor and Stuart dynasties is Hampton Court, originally built by Cardinal Wolsey but diplomatically handed over to Henry VIII in 1529. The king remodelled much of the building, spending over £62,000 (about £18 million today) on it in ten years to create one of the most modern and sophisticated palaces in Europe. The great kitchens are frequently used to produce historic Tudor feasts, and interpreters in costume are often on site. Much of Hampton Court was rebuilt by Wren for William III. This king's Privy Garden has recently been restored, and the famous maze, laid out in the 1790s in hornbeam and replanted in yew in the 1960s, still baffles visitors.

Audley End House in Essex, a palace in effect, cost its builder, the 1st Earl of Suffolk and James I's Lord Treasurer, the vast sum of £200,000. One of the finest Jacobean houses, it is complemented by the alterations of Robert Adam and 'Capability' Brown (pages 133–4).

Recreating the past

'My two older sons were really shy and in awe of the king, but my youngest went up to him and asked him straight out where his wife was, and which one she was.'

BELOW: Henry VIII holds court at Dover Castle in a recreation of his royal visits there. Magnificent costume, pageantry and authentic musical instruments all contribute to the atmosphere of a great Tudor spectacle.

THE TUDOR AND STUART ERAS offer plenty of opportunities for very diverse recreations of life and events. The Civil War is the focus of much re-enactment, often at sites where actual battles and skirmishes took place. The great battles of Marston Moor, Edgehill and Naseby are performed with well-researched details of dress, armour, weaponry, camp life and food; documents of the time give valuable information about formations, tactics and the unfolding of events. Physical settings are an important factor, revealing the influence of terrain on strategy and outcome. At Naseby, where the hedges that hampered troop movements still exist, the lie of the land prevented the armies from seeing each other until they were at close quarters, when it became clear that the royalists were heavily outnumbered.

Time of day was also significant, as was the weather – harder for re-enactors to reproduce. Marston Moor was fought in the late afternoon, in the middle of a thunderstorm, which dampened powder and made musket misfires more likely. In a dramatic reversal, Fairfax and Cromwell rallied their cavalry to trap the royalists in a pincer movement; the Marquis of Newcastle's Whitecoats fought to the last man in gathering gloom. About 6000 royalists were killed or captured.

However, battles are only one aspect of recreations from this period. Tudor and Stuart buildings offer authentic backdrops for recreating historic royal progresses – complete with plays, feasts and stately dances – as well as ordinary daily life. This, too, can be played out in the grand houses of the period. Kentwell Hall in Suffolk, one of England's finest Tudor moated houses, was built in the first half of the 16th century on the profits of the wool trade. Its modern owners open it to the public for part of the year, when it provides a setting for large-scale recreations of Tudor life by men, women and children. Their recreations are often set in a specific year and reflect historic events that directly affected day-to-day life, such as the riots of 1549 against the enclosure of common land in Suffolk. Interpretations at Kentwell offer a real opportunity to get close to daily life in the past, and show the impact of the wider world on small, local communities.

ROYAL PROGRESSES

Kings and queens expected only the best when they honoured one of their courtiers with their presence, and re-enactments of their progresses are magnificent events. When Henry VIII and his court visited Dover Castle in March 1539, the empty medieval castle was

temporarily transformed into elaborate royal apartments: the rich trappings contrasted with cold grey stone, concealing the castle as it normally would have been – empty, echoing and uncomfortable. An exhibition in the castle shows some of the splendid furniture, hangings and equipment that arrived to make ready for a visit by the king, and the enormous trunks and other baggage needed to transport it all.

It is unlikely that the real Henry would have recognized Walmer Castle as it is today – a comfortable official home for the Lord Warden of the Cinque Ports rather than a severe military structure. In a recent interpretation of his visit, the king consented to be entertained by the 16th-century Lord Warden and his lady although, very aware of his importance, he berated his host for laying his table with earthenware vessels rather than silver. Henry could also be gracious, however; he held audiences with his subjects, proclaiming to them in a deep, booming voice that suited his larger-than-life persona. It was an impressive spectacle: the Tudor courtiers were glamorously attired and Henry's gloriously embroidered clothes were complemented by a magnificent codpiece. The overseer of building at Henry's new castles was also present, but without a codpiece as he had just ridden down from Sandown Castle – display giving way to practicality! Whole families joined in the period dances led by Tudor courtiers, lending fun and laughter to the historical authenticity behind the event.

The courtly progresses of Elizabeth I around her kingdom are commemorated by the many houses that proudly advertise that she slept there. Like her father, she was not always an easy guest; she let

ABOVE: Sir Edward Ryngley, overseer of construction work on Henry VIII's new castles at Sandown, Deal and Walmer, in attendance at the king's visit to nearby Dover. His clothes are less flamboyant than those of the monarch and his court, but still show a richness befitting his status, with fur linings and slashed decoration, enhanced by an impressive chain of office.

RIGHT: Kenilworth Castle in Warwickshire, with its recreated Tudor garden in the foreground. Built in the early 12th century, Kenilworth took centre stage during the mid-16th century – acquired by the Dudley family, it was sequestered by the crown when John Dudley was executed for trying to put his daughter-in-law, Lady Jane Grey, on the throne. His elder son Robert, however, became a favourite of Elizabeth I and the castle was duly returned.

Sir Nicholas Bacon know in no uncertain terms how deficient she found the welcome he had laid on for her at Old Gorhambury House. Yet aspiring courtiers were still willing to take the risk, as a successful royal visit was a great investment towards patronage and influence. Kenilworth Castle in Warwickshire, a gift from the queen to Robert Dudley, was the site of one of Elizabeth's most magnificent progresses which has passed into legend. A fabled extravaganza was enacted for her there in July 1575, when for 19 days Dudley, whom she had created Earl of Leicester in 1563, laid on splendid festivities including bear-baiting, hunting, music, speeches in Latin and a play about the massacre of the Danes in 1002. The continuous round of plays, masques and dances was punctuated by elaborate feasts. Exotic pageantry on the lake featured the legendary Lady of the Lake on a floating island ablaze with torches, and it is claimed that the noise of

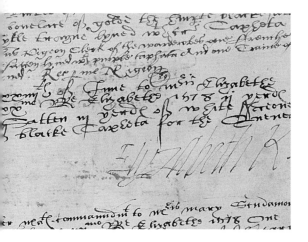

ABOVE: An order for taffeta fabric, dated 1578 and signed by Elizabeth herself. The queen loved rich clothes, and used their impact to shape her iconic role.

RIGHT: A royal procession enters the gardens at Kenilworth, treading in the footsteps of one from over 400 years ago.

drums, fifes, trumpets, gun salutes and fireworks could be heard 20 miles away. At its climax, trumpets summoned the queen to the lakeshore to behold Arion riding on the back of an immense dolphin, 7 m (23 feet) in length, with six musicians concealed in its belly. The young William Shakespeare is said to have been there and to have used his memories of the occasion in *A Midsummer Night's Dream*. The whole event cost Dudley the prodigious sum of £1000 a day, on top of the expense he had to incur for an extensive makeover of the castle.

Even a ruined structure such as Kenilworth can be brought dramatically to life by recreations of such occasions, with costumes, music and food of the period contributing to the festive atmosphere.

OPPOSITE, ABOVE AND BELOW LEFT: The queen's fascination with theatrical display was reflected in the elaborate costumes of her court. Rich fabrics, delicate embroidery and tumbling lace adorned the clothes of men and women, and bright colours were high fashion.

ABOVE: Queen Elizabeth I, flanked by Leicester and other attentive courtiers, watches a play performed in her honour at Kenilworth. Pageants, masques and plays were required entertainment for royal progresses, as were dancing, feasting, mock battles and fireworks.

Interpreters draw on evidence in letters, accounts and other documents of the time to show how the occasion unfolded, and the expenditure was clearly vast. A fashionable wardrobe was also essential for courtiers on such occasions, and like their predecessors, the interpreters are resplendent in rich silks, taffeta, velvet and lace.

Many houses were built or refurbished in the hope of welcoming the queen and her vast retinue. Theobalds, Holdenby and Longleat were some of the many that were transformed. So was Kirby Hall in Northamptonshire, intended by its owner, Sir Christopher Hatton, as a shrine to his royal patroness; but she never went there. James I and Anne of Denmark, however, did visit on several occasions.

Charles I continued the tradition. In 1634 he went with his queen, Henrietta Maria, on a progress to Bolsover Castle in Derbyshire, recently renovated by its owner, Sir William Cavendish, a leading figure at court. The long gallery and an external staircase were added for the visit, and the dramatist Ben Jonson was commissioned to compose a masque, *Love's Welcome at Bolsover*. This lavish spectacular, charged with a sense of place and occasion, was performed in a string of locations round the castle, including the new

LEFT AND ABOVE: The Pillar Parlour at Bolsover, originally called the 'lower dining room', held the masques and allegorical entertainments for which the Little Castle was designed. The Parlour probably played host to Charles I and Henrietta Maria, whose visit of 1634 was recently recreated on the site (above). The original panelling and decoration survived until 1976; it has been recreated from a small surviving piece to the left of the fireplace.

ABOVE: The splendour of Audley End House caught Charles II's eye and a recreation of his visit to its owner, the Earl of Suffolk, displayed all the glamour of the Restoration court. The king's acquisitiveness ran to more than buildings, and he also showered attention on his young mistress, Nell Gwynne. Her hair is fashionably dressed in soft thick ringlets, allowed to fall in numerous curls around the face (detail, above).

long gallery. It was preceded and followed by enormous banquets during which, among other delicacies such as sturgeon, 41 different types of birds were eaten. The accounts survive and show that they ate 30 each of swans, peacocks and turkeys, 10 dozen geese, 30 dozen capons, 8 dozen gulls and 20 bitterns. The tablecloths alone cost £160, and the entire bill came to nearly £15,000, which left Cavendish 'plunged in debt' and gloomy about his prospects.

This event has been recreated (on a more manageable scale) at Bolsover, blending elaborate ceremony with authentic entertainment. The king and queen were greeted by Cavendish and his wife, and treated to a performance of the Prologue of Jonson's masque, after which they gave gracious audience to the spectators and granted royal favours. The court party tasted wine and comfits, accompanied by the music of lutes, recorders and other instruments of the time, followed by dances to the pipe and tabor. Charles I, always a very formal monarch, stood aloof, but Henrietta Maria took part, as did the courtiers, who encouraged the watching 'commoners' to join in too.

Progresses resumed after the restoration of the monarchy in 1660, when Charles II returned from exile in France to establish a court renowned for its grandeur and decadence. A recently recreated progress at Audley End was based on a historical visit by the 'Merrie Monarch', after Charles II had expressed an interest in buying the house, which was convenient for horse-racing at nearby Newmarket. The Earl of Suffolk was keen to entertain his royal guest and show him round his prospective purchase, the upkeep of which was more than a little burdensome. Catherine of Braganza, Charles II's queen, was absent, but his young mistress, Nell Gwynne, accompanied him, revelling in her new status and joining the king in his favourite dance, 'Cuckolds all awry', played on the pipe and tabor.

All grand Stuart clothing was rich and elaborate, with much use of silk, lace and bright colours, but the underlying design of doublet, hose and knee breeches remained much as it had for centuries – until the Restoration. Male dress then changed radically, with the first appearance of the three-piece suit, in the form of a long coat, a long waistcoat and breeches. Another new fashion was wigs: Charles I did not wear one but his son did – luxuriantly. At the recreated Audley End progress, it was notable that Charles II was resplendent in the new style of dress, while his older, more conservative host, the Earl of Suffolk, wore a more traditional costume.

FASHIONS IN FOOD AND DRINK

Charles II and Catherine of Braganza were both partial to tea, a new and fashionable drink in European courts. It is thought to have arrived in England in the 1650s, when it was sold from the apothecary's shop as a luxury item alongside rare spices. Tea-drinking rapidly became popular in aristocratic circles. The valuable leaves were kept in locked caddies, presided over by the lady of the house, who controlled their consumption. Tea cups were tiny bowls, befitting the costly contents.

Food and drink were important in most social occasions and 'receipt books' are evocative documents of domestic life. They were kept by women with households – who had to be apothecaries and nurses as well as wives, mothers and cooks, even if they were wealthy, with servants for the hard work – and passed down through families. Lady Elinor Fettiplace's book, from the early 17th century, has been translated into a working modern recipe book by Hilary Spurling. Her magnificently random collection of recipes for food, medicines, preserves, cooking techniques and more reminds us that everything, from baking bread and brewing beer to preserving fruit and distilling herbs in the stillroom, had to be done at home, The receipt book was copied out by a scribe and annotated in Lady Elinor's hand, including notes on Sir Walter Raleigh's two recipes for tobacco-based cordials.

'Let yor butter bee scaldinge hott in yor pan and powre in yor Batter, as yt doth begin to bake stir yt wth a knife untill yt will frye wthout stickinge …'

LADY FETTIPLACE'S OMELETTE,
[AN EARLY 17TH-CENTURY RECIPE]

The tea ceremony in Stuart times

1 Tea, the new and exotic import from the East, required a whole new array of serving vessles. Porcelain tea pots, derived from ceramic kettles, and tiny bowls reflect tea's Chinese origins in their shape and decoration.

2 The Countess of Suffolk herself prepares the beverage, attended by a maid bearing hot water in a jug. The leaves, brought from a locked caddy to prevent theft, are carefully measured into the warmed pot.

3 Hot, steaming water is added to the pot, and its lid replaced. The leaves are allowed to infuse for a few minutes, then the Countess pours the sweet smelling liquid into the small, translucent Chinese bowls.

4 The Countess sips her tea carefully from the handleless dish. A luxury at this time, tea was drunk black and in small quantities that reflected its value. It was believed to have many beneficial medicinal properties.

RIGHT AND BELOW: People from various levels of society feature in the Weald and Downland Museum's recreation of life in a Sussex parish in 1626. The Clares, a prosperous yeoman farming family at Pendean Farm, employ labourers to bring in the harvest (right), bound in authentically shaped sheaves. Samuel Walker (below), tenant of Poplar Cottage, makes his living from the woodland on the edge of the parish. The event follows the families, their activities and concerns, and all characters are willing to talk to spectators about the lives they portray.

Food and how it was prepared provide intriguing insights into everyday life. Chicken could be roasted on a spit turned by a little dog on a treadmill. People ate 'umble pie' made from entrails ('umbles'), or made joke pies baked blind and filled with live birds or a snake. Hints for cooking pike included 'rub his skin off while he lives' or – more practically – 'Take a male pike alive and splat him in halves.'

Samuel Pepys' diaries are a fine source of details about food later in the century, including some memorable disasters. Preserving could fail horribly, as when Pepys was given a sturgeon in early May 1662; he kept it in a pickle until the end of June, when it arrived at table with little worms creeping all over it. In such straits,it was possible to summon a 'take-away', but Pepys' servants once forgot to remove food from bowls carrying the real cook's name, to his great embarrassment!

RECREATING RURAL LIFE

Most of the buildings central to rural life in the 17th century have long disappeared or been absorbed into later structures. Some have

been rescued by living museums such as the Weald and Downland Open Air Museum in Sussex, where they are brought to life again by interpreters. Every year members of the History Re-enactment Workshop turn the museum's houses into homes, casting themselves as real people of the 1620s and re-enacting the details of their lives.

Richard and Katharine Clare, for example, play a yeoman farmer and his wife, living at Pendean Farm. Among their preoccupations are the extra help needed at harvest time, what is best for their children and how to combine the additional workload with Richard's parish duties. Their servant, Charity Simmons, lives at Pendean with her four-year-old son, Robert, and the Clares are also caring for Anice Samuels, daughter of the local bailiff who has been called away from the parish on business. Charity is worrying whether the time is right to 'breech' her young son (that is, to exchange his babyish garments for boy's clothes). The tenants at Poplar Cottage, the coppicer Samuel

ABOVE: The inhabitants of Pendean Farm, originally a small yeoman farmhouse built to the south of Midhurst, Sussex, in 1609. The Clare family and their servants wear similar styles of clothing, made of homespun wool and linen, as they all engaged in work on the farm and in the house. Adults and children, too, were similarly dressed, once young boys were taken out of their infant dresses and 'breeched'.

Walker and his wife Hannah, hope for more children but worry about whether his trade is good enough to give them a reasonable living.

Real people in real situations – interpreted by modern enthusiasts who make and wear 17th-century clothing, act out family situations and as far as possible 'become' people of the 1620s. There are only a few concessions to modern times, of which the main one is language. Authentic pronunciation and sentence structure made it harder for the interpreters to stay in character and created a barrier between themselves and their audiences. The interpreters now use modern pronunciation and a watered-down sentence structure that allows them to sound sufficiently different but not impenetrable. Such concessions illustrate how hard it is to step back completely into the mindset of the past, but at the same time how fascinating it is to try.

An authentic picture of life in southern England in the year 1642 is the purpose of the Gosport Living History Society. It has created the village of Little Woodham in the parish of Rowner near Gosport as it would have been at the outbreak of the Civil War. On certain days through the year Little Woodham is peopled by interpreters in costume; they focus on the village's day-to-day activities and social life in that year, despite the momentous political events about to unfold. Extensive research into people living at the time, using parish registers, wills, muster lists and court records, makes it possible to recreate life

'It's hard work, with everything being done by hand and no modern equipment. Sometimes you wonder how they ever coped, with their extended families and servants and visitors all living cramped together in a small cottage. But you also feel really part of a community, sharing all that went on around you.'

RIGHT: Hannah Walker, the coppicer's wife, prepares a meal at Poplar Cottage, Weald and Downland Museum. The cottage originally stood near Steyning, Sussex, and is broadly contemporary though it cannot be exactly dated. In 1626, rural people ate food that was home-grown, organic and seasonal, and everything was done by hand with very basic equipment.

in this self-contained community. Here people continued with their ordinary tasks and occupied themselves with the ever-present concerns of growing, storing and preparing food, providing against the dark and cold of winter, building adequate shelters, making clothes for themselves and their families, and caring for the young, old or sick.

The buildings of Little Woodham were originally constructed in the 1980s for a Civil War re-enactment. Too good to pull down, they have become the local village setting, as authentic as possible, that exists today. The society is run by volunteers who make their costumes and in turn lend new members garments and patterns to create their own. During the re-enactments they work on the buildings, make lace, card wool and adapt the activities and events on the site to reflect the changing seasons. The siege of Portsmouth at the start of the Civil War brings a few soldiers to the village, but the emphasis remains very much on daily life in this area of England at that specific time.

RECREATING THE CIVIL WAR

The 16th century saw few battles on British soil, though Henry VIII had to fight the Scots more than once; the 17th century saw too many, as the Civil War famously pitted family members against one another as allegiances shifted and evolved. Weaponry and armour changed significantly over the period, as did the shape of military action. Those

ABOVE: A new, reed-thatched roof is put on to a house in Little Woodham, which recreates village life in 1642. Thatching was a highly skilled job, starting at the eaves and building up to the ridge. Thatch, the most common roofing material for rural buildings since medieval times, was both warm and effective against rain, though vulnerable to fire and pests.

fighting at Flodden in 1513 used essentially medieval weaponry, though powerful, two-handed pikes and bills, up to 5.5 m (18 feet) long, had replaced the longbow as their use grew more effective. Pikes were still formidable weapons in the Civil War, but artillery played a much greater role, and even ordinary soldiers now carried muskets. The smoke of musket volleys was a new hazard of warfare, obscuring the field and assaulting eyes and lungs with a bitter, acrid smell.

Muskets were also unreliable weapons, requiring drill and discipline to load and fire properly – not easy in the heat of battle. Some men had reputations as 'hard men', impervious to musket balls, a power supposedly acquired through drinking special concoctions. In reality, if powder was not properly compressed by the ramrod, the ball would not achieve maximum velocity – such 'slow' bullets might inflict little damage. Those relying on potions must have had a rude shock if they encountered a properly prepared and fired musket ball.

RIGHT: The New Model Army waits to engage in the battle of Kirby Hall Farm. The drummer was a vital member of the regiment, signalling the advance and keeping the momentum going; he had to be a fit young man to keep up while carrying his heavy drums. The rules of modern recreations remove the sheer brutality of hand-to-hand combat, and fears of wounding or death, but there is still trepidation and the rush of adrenalin as combat approaches.

'The rule was that if a pike touched your arm or leg, you should fall down, dead or wounded. Sometimes we were told to fall down at a particular point in the skirmish. At least we didn't have to face the horrors of real wounds, with awful treatment that was probably useless anyway.'

OPPOSITE: The Parliamentarian New Model Army battle against Royalist forces for control of Kirby Hall Farm, a building specially reconstructed for Civil War re-enactments. Parliamentarian troops wear the red uniform adopted by the New Model Army when it was formed in 1645 – the first consistent uniform. 'Bodies' sprinkle the foreground, as some re-enactors are ordered to 'play dead' for authenticity's sake.

Contrary to popular opinion, not all Royalists dressed in lace and bright colours; nor did all Roundheads wear dull greys and browns. In fact, both sides looked similar, and soldiers wore mixtures of colours and styles, depending on the equipment and uniform provided by their leaders, or that they could obtain for themselves. Some regiments had specific uniforms, but no consistent approach defined allegiance; two regiments known as the Whitecoats might be found on opposite sides. Re-enactors of Civil War battles adopt the distinguishing devices of their forebears: the Parliamentarians at Edgehill wore orange scarves and the royalists red ones, while at Marston Moor the Parliamentarian soldiers placed white cloths in their hats for identification. The New Model Army, founded in 1645, first adopted the red coat that became the British military standard for the next two and a half centuries.

The Tudor and Stuart centuries offer re-enactors varied and splendid possibilities. Some events celebrate the splendid fashions of the period, especially the rich fabrics and glorious colours favoured by the wealthy. But it is also fascinating to explore how more ordinary people lived: how they grew crops and kept livestock, how they built their homes and fed their families. Battles show the beginning of a more modern warfare and offer marvellous opportunities for research and recreation. In centuries so full of familiar, high-profile events, it is particularly important to explore what it really meant to live then.

The first King George was the Elector of Hanover before Queen Anne's lack of surviving heirs gave him the crown. George spoke little English and much preferred Hanover, where he died in 1727, on one of his frequent visits. Yet the era to which he and

LIFE IN GEORGIAN TIMES

his successors gave their names now seems archetypally British – a time of elegance and culture, in which creative energy jostled with radical ideas in politics and science. The delights of great country houses and landscaped gardens, Palladian architecture and picaresque novels were balanced by wars and revolutions, poverty and epidemics, and the dawn of the modern industrial age.

6

Approaching Georgian times

We associate the Georgian age with pleasure and cultured leisure – a time of flourishing theatre, music and stimulating conversation in coffee houses; of 'Farmer George' and the foppish Prince Regent; of taking the waters amid the splendours of Bath; of grand tours and life as it was lived in the novels of Jane Austen. Yet it was also a period of intellectual ferment, with new scientific enquiry leading to huge leaps forward in discovery and understanding, and industrialization starting to change the ways in which people had lived for centuries. The legacy of the classical past might dominate houses of a cultured aristocracy; but the underside to such magnificence was the immense poverty that still held much of the population in its grip.

It was not a peaceful time. George II was the last British king to lead his troops into battle – at Dettingen in Bavaria in 1743 – and George III's reign saw the American War of Independence and the loss of the American colonies. The romantic legend surrounding Charles Edward Stuart ('Bonnie Prince Charlie') and the Jacobite uprisings in 1715 and 1745 conceals the cruelty with which the rebels were treated after the defeat at Culloden, and the later destruction of the Highland way of life in the Clearances. The French Revolution led to political turmoil as the established order of society, never before so radically challenged, was rapidly overthrown; and the Napoleonic

Wars in Europe got perilously close to home, with an invasion by Napoleon appearing all too likely. The heroes of the time, particularly Nelson and Wellington, still resonate in popular history today, with Trafalgar Square and Waterloo Station in London commemorating the period's great naval and military victories.

It was the age of red-coated soldiers, big dresses and big hair, savage caricatures by Gillray and Rowlandson and Hogarth's satirical depictions of urban depravity. Industry was growing apace and the enclosure movement was changing the face of the countryside. The 18th century seems somehow nearer to our world than what went before: Georgians played cricket; the chattering classes worried about declining standards in the press; architecture and design were great status symbols; and a cult of celebrity was emerging, with the glamour and notoriety of figures such as Byron and Shelley, the Prince Regent and Napoleon. We can still visit the art collection at the Courtauld, endowed by descendants of the Huguenot family who settled in Spitalfields, London, at this time. Yet not all Georgian towns were prosperous and life was precarious for many of their inhabitants. Infant mortality remained high, smallpox was a killer and judicial punishments brutal in the extreme. This society still burned women at the stake, yet could also build the glorious Royal Crescent at Bath.

ABOVE: Chiswick House was built in neo-Palladian style in 1729. A contemporary described Burlington's palace of culture and leisure as 'too little to live in, and too large to hang to one's watch'.

BELOW: The indictment of legendary highwayman Dick Turpin for stealing a mare (his famous horse Black Bess) and a filly foal from Thomas Creasy in 1739. It can be seen at the National Archives.

Visiting Georgian sites

MANY 18TH-CENTURY BUILDINGS are still part of daily life. Elegant towns remain living communities, and Georgian houses of merchants and artisans are people's homes. Others are offices, such as Somerset House in London, rebuilt in the 18th century to hold government offices and learned societies, and now magnificently restored. The mills and canals of a burgeoning industrial age changed the face of town and country, while new defences were built and old ones strengthened against the Jacobites and Napoleon. Country houses, urban crescents, turnpike roads and sailing ships all give insight into this volatile, rapidly changing century, and the people who lived in it.

DEFENCES ON LAND AND SEA

Carlisle Castle is a grim place even today. How much more grim must it have been for the Jacobite soldiers, taken prisoner when the brutal Duke of Cumberland recaptured Carlisle from Charles Edward Stuart's forces. The prisoners were herded into small, lightless cells,

BELOW: Nelson's flagship, HMS *Victory*, now in dry dock at Portsmouth, was built in the 1760s at Chatham. It cost £63,176, the equivalent of building an aircraft carrier today, and delights visitors who can board the ship and join in the interactive 'Trafalgar!' experience.

where they were reduced to licking the walls for moisture. Those cramped cells are still there, with their licking stones, the walls worn away and scarred with holes where chains were once attached. On a wet June day, it was a shivery experience to be alone there, imagining them filled with hundreds of starving men, aware that their fate – as indeed proved to be the case – was likely to be the hangman's noose.

After Culloden in 1746, the Jacobite cause was dead in all but legend, though fortified border towns such as Carlisle and Berwick-upon-Tweed provided a reminder of the turbulent past. The barracks at Berwick, probably based on Nicholas Hawksmoor's design and built between 1717 and 1725, were a response to the Jacobite uprising of the 'Old Pretender'. Today they form the backdrop for recreations and exhibitions that bring to life details of 18th-century soldiers' lives.

The threat of invasion rose again later in the century, this time from Napoleonic France. On clear days from the heights above Dover, the white cliffs of Calais appear as if on the other side of a lake – far too close for the liking of the military, who built a string of Martello

ABOVE: A recent recruit into the army of George III, not yet entitled to wear the redcoat of the fully trained soldier. Demand for men for both army and navy was huge in the 18th century, and underhand methods of trapping young men into 'taking the king's shilling' were not uncommon. The event at Lyddington Bede House recreated recruitment tactics as well as authentic military clothing and weapons at the time of the American War of Independence (1775–83).

RIGHT: Letters can bring us close to the drama of actual events. This account of how pressed men escaped from a sloop, the *Thunder*, on 18 October 1740 adds that one of the Press Gang drowned in the fight, showing the real desperation of men brought unwillingly on board ship.

towers along the south coast as a bulwark against French landings. Over 40 still remain, with an impressive sequence between Hythe and Dymchurch, where the tower sits incongruously in a modern seaside resort. It is in the care of English Heritage and open to the public.

During the 18th century naval power was vital to Britain's security, particularly during the Napoleonic Wars. Chatham's naval dockyard built and launched 125 ships between 1700 and 1815, and press gangs terrorized coastal towns to recruit men and boys to serve on 'ships of the line'. After the working site closed in 1984, surviving buildings were transformed into the evocative Historic Dockyard, the world's most complete dockyard from the Age of Sail. Most buildings at Chatham today date from the 18th century, including the vast working ropery, 346 m (¼ of a mile) long. The famous Wooden Walls gallery recreates the sites, sounds and smells of the dockyard in 1758 through the experience of an apprentice starting work there; it includes a tour of some of the 26 trades needed to build the *Valiant*, a 74-gun warship.

The most famous ship built at Chatham was Nelson's flagship, HMS *Victory*, now in dry dock at Portsmouth's Historic Dockyard. The interactive recreation of 'Trafalgar!' allows visitors to experience

ABOVE: The Wooden Walls adventure at Chatham recounts the first day at work there in 1758 of young apprentice William Crockwell. After a tour of the dockyard and its trades, including dusty sawpits and the fiery anchor smithy, William visits the gun deck of the *Valiant*, a 74-gun 'ship of the line' about to sail against the French fleet. The people in this interpretation really did exist, and have been researched in naval and dockyard records.

LEFT: The working, ¼-mile-long ropery at Chatham Historic Dockyard still produces the rope once vital for the navy. Every Georgian sailing ship needed 20 miles of rope for its rigging alone, and much of the present-day output, produced by master ropemakers, is used for replicas of sailing ships.

RIGHT: Appuldurcombe House, now only a shell, was once the grandest house on the Isle of Wight. The east front, with its projecting pavilions, is unusual for the 18th century and was probably influenced by innovative French château architecture. The grounds of Appuldurcombe were designed by Lancelot 'Capability' Brown towards the end of the 18th century.

BELOW: Dawn mist hangs over the Long Water and baroque pavilion at Wrest Park in Bedfordshire. The gardens, rare examples of early 18th-century style, rely on revelation and mystery for impact: a mix of open space, sheltered woodland walks and reflective expanses of water surprises at every turn.

the thrilling sights and sounds on *Victory*'s gundeck as the fleet goes into action. A naval centre for centuries, Portsmouth is one of Britain's most fortified towns. It contains a well preserved 18th-century fort, Fort Cumberland – now English Heritage's Centre for Archaeology.

COUNTRY HOUSES AND GARDENS

The country houses of the 18th century, set within carefully crafted landscapes, are some of England's most splendid sites. Architectural elegance is enhanced by surrounding gardens and parks that are glories in themselves, combining classical inspiration with the celebration of a natural 'wilderness'. Great landscape designers such as William Kent, Humphry Repton and Lancelot 'Capability' Brown re-interpreted the settings of country houses, subtly manipulating existing parkland into a new, harmonious whole.

Brown's energy was prodigious and many of the grand gardens we visit today are his work, from Appuldurcombe to Blenheim and Audley End. He dug away tons of soil for his lakes and water features, literally moving mountains, or at least mounds, if necessary, and thinking nothing of replanting fully mature trees. Stowe, where Brown worked under William Kent, is a great Georgian landscape garden, with lakes and rivers, valleys and vistas dotted with allegorical temples and monuments. Under Brown's aegis a river at Blenheim Palace was dammed to create twin lakes, and he revitalized the setting of the great Jacobean house at Audley End (page 110) while one of the century's leading architects, Robert Adam, remodelled the interior.

Even more radical changes were taking place in architecture and design, reflecting the influence of classical buildings seen by the aristocracy on their grand tours of Europe. Chiswick House, built in the 1720s, was highly innovative, reflecting Lord Burlington's enthusiasm for Andrea Palladio, a 16th-century Italian architect. Palladian villas seem now typical of Georgian style, their harmonious proportions and calm austerity keynotes to a graceful, confident age.

Robert Adam's designs for Kenwood House were also innovative; they include the north and south façades and the great library, where mirrored recesses play tricks with the visitor's gaze. He transformed Osterley Park, to the west of London, into an elegant, neoclassical villa. Kedleston Hall in Derbyshire also has interiors of his design, complete and unaltered, as well as a fine collection of furniture and paintings. Bowood House in Wiltshire, site of a famous Adam library, combines 18th-century grandeur with its progressive spirit: in 1774 Joseph Priestley, tutor to the son of the house, discovered oxygen, which he called 'dephlogisticated air', in its small working laboratory.

Elegant urban life

Just walking around certain towns, whether grand or more ordinary, brings us close to Georgian life. Fashion overtook Bath in the 18th century, and the small spa town inside Roman walls rapidly expanded; by the 1750s it had become England's leading pleasure resort for the well-to-do. Bath was a planned town, and it looks much as it did 250 years ago: sweeping terraces and crescents, glowing golden stone, attractive public parks and gardens. More than anywhere, this city conjures up the poise and elegance of fashionable Georgian life. The Pump Rooms still function as a place to take tea and the health-giving waters – they can be sampled there at a drinking fountain.

After Bath, Stamford in Lincolnshire is one of the most complete and exquisite stone-built Georgian towns. On a small and local scale, Deal, just south of Sandwich in Kent, also conveys a sense of the

ABOVE: The beautifully restored interiors of Marble Hill House feature an impressive collection of early Georgian paintings, as well as authentic furniture and ornaments from the period. From such evidence, interpreters can learn more about the details of leisured 18th-century life and recreate them in living history events.

OPPOSITE: Pulteney Bridge, one of only three bridges lined with shops in the world, is, surprisingly, Robert Adam's only structure in Bath. Although when completed in the 1770s it initially led on to meadows, it has become an enduring symbol of the city, famous in Georgian times for its spa, social activities and provincial marriage broking.

'I really believe I shall always be talking of Bath, when I am at home again – I do like it so very much. If I could but have papa and mamma, and the rest of them here, I suppose I should be too happy! … Oh! Who can ever be tired of Bath?'

JANE AUSTEN, *NORTHANGER ABBEY*

BELOW: Buildings at the royal spa of Tunbridge Wells offer an authentic backdrop for colourful 18th-century fashions. Elaborate hats and parasols were *de rigueur*.

period. Hundreds of artisans' cottages still stand on narrow, winding streets, where corner buildings have wedges cut out to allow carts to turn. Evidence of smuggling lingers in the houses: rat runs still cut through attics and ingenious hiding-places emerge during building work, such as the box buried under a basement floor, its top concealed by old fireplace flags. The cottages and narrow streets became slums and barely escaped 'modernization', but their survival means that on a snowy winter's night ir is easy to imagine oneself in the 18th century.

Many areas of London retain a flavour of the Georgian city. Elegant houses in Spitalfields, once those of Huguenot weavers, were until recently decrepit and empty. When Dennis Severs bought 18 Folgate Street in 1979, he was alone in a street of warehouses and boarded-up buildings. He moved in with a bedroll, chamber pot and candle, and slept in each room to discover its character before bringing the house to life as the home of the fictitious Jervis family. Visitors encounter 18th-century people who are heard, smelled and imagined, but never seen. Clothes hang over chairs, the mistress has just had tea, the chamber pot waits to be emptied, a child fumbles at a door … It is all in all an extraordinary recreation of daily life, called by Severs a reincarnation. The Spitalfields Trust took over the house on Severs' death, and now open it to the public in the spirit of its creator.

Recreating the past

MANY OF BRITAIN'S LIVING MUSEUMS feature 18th-century buildings and activities, showing how ordinary people lived in the country and emerging towns. Georgian re-enactment also reflects the century's variety, offering all kinds of roles, military and civilian, male and female, each requiring flattering costumes that are fun to wear. Bright colours, cascading hairstyles or wigs, splendid hats – interpreters who wear clothes of this time say that their formality and complexity force them to walk with a sweep and a swagger, to keep their heads high and their shoulders back – the costume imposes arrogance on them.

AN EARLY INDUSTRIAL AGE

The Georgian period saw the beginning of large-scale industrialization in Britain, and Ironbridge Gorge in Shropshire is probably the best-known industrial heritage site. In the 18th century, Ironbridge – then called Coalbrookdale – was the most industrialized place on earth. Coal and clay mines were juxtaposed with iron-, brick- and tileworks, forges and foundries, and at its centre stood the Iron Bridge itself, erected in 1779 and the first of its size ever built in this material. Today the Gorge is a World Heritage Site and an innovative museum. It has

ABOVE: Abraham Darby cast the Iron Bridge at his ironworks at Coalbrookdale, now called Ironbridge and a World Heritage Site. These beams are set into the original blast furnace there to commemorate his work. The Severn Valley can justly claim to be the cradle of the Industrial Revolution, producing not just iron but china and decorated ceramic tiles. Today it retains the relics of its industrial infrastructure.

RIGHT: This replica of the world's first successful steam engine, built by Thomas Newcomen in 1712, was painstakingly recreated at the Black Country Living Museum in 1986. Little is known of Thomas Newcomen, and no portrait of him exists, but he was an early pioneer of the steam engines that powered the Industrial Revolution.

TOP: Richard Trevithick was an early advocate of the 'dangerous' practice of using high-pressure steam to propel a vehicle. A working replica of his 1802 prototype for the Coalbrookdale ironworks (where it ran on iron rails) is at Blists Hill (top). A similar engine later won a bet for a Welsh ironmaster when it hauled 25 tons of iron plus 70 passengers.

ABOVE: Living history events feature people from all levels of society. The hardships of ordinary life in an emerging industrial area – poverty, poor housing, long hours of repetitive work – are clearly portrayed by this interpreter.

displays, exhibitions and living history on several sites, recreating the beginnings of industry and ways of life for those living amidst it all during the 18th and 19th centuries.

In contrast to the leisured existence of society's upper echelons, conditions in many of the new factories and mills, and the towns that grew up around them, were often very poor. Child labour was cheap and hours long, although a few enlightened employers, such as David Dale and his son-in-law Robert Owen, built model villages for their workforce. Their employees had fair wages, free health care and well-built tenement blocks with wash-rooms and communal buildings, including a school, at New Lanark in Scotland. Today it is possible to stay in the conserved buildings of New Lanark, Scotland's first industrial World Heritage Site, and to enjoy the countryside around as well as events and occasions such as fairs and dances.

Meticulously reconstructed workers' cottages from the late 18th century can be seen at the Black Country Living Museum, Dudley, which celebrates the heritage of this industrial heartland. A small terrace of six cottages at the Museum of Welsh Life was built by the ironmaster Richard Crawshay for ironstone miners at Merthyr Tydfil at the beginning of the 19th century. The houses have been displayed to illustrate different periods of their history, from 1805 up to 1985.

Many open-air museums around the country feature structures from the early industrial age – often in the form of original buildings that have been moved to the site. The Museum of Welsh Life has a small woollen mill, originally built in Llanwrtyd, Powys, in 1760; it contains probably the only spinning jack of its type still working, dating from *c*.1830. The mill still makes Welsh shawls and blankets (*carthenni*), often seen stretched out on the tenter frame outside.

The Black Country Living Museum features a working, full-scale replica of the 1712 Newcomen Engine, based on a local engraving of 1719. The 'fire engine', as it was originally known, consists of a solid brick building with a wooden beam extending through one wall. Rods hanging from the beam's outside end operate pumps in the bottom of the mine shaft to raise water to the surface. The engine itself is relatively simple – a boiler, cylinder and piston, and operating valves. Also of 18th-century construction is the Dudley Tunnel Branch of the Birmingham canal system, which surrounds the museum on three sides. The authentic infrastructure includes old lime kilns, a lifting bridge and a working boat dock typical of Black Country canals.

Roads were also improving, through new turnpikes and tolls. The Chiltern Open Air Museum has a toll-house from 1826, built on the London–Oxford road for £500. The Weald and Downland Museum has one of 1807, its gates recreated from a 19th-century photograph.

RURAL WAYS OF LIFE

Much of the population was still rural, although enclosure of common land and high food prices in the Napoleonic Wars (maintained by the notorious Corn Laws) meant that poverty was endemic. The main building of the Museum of Rural Life at Gressenhall is an 18th-century workhouse, where actual events are re-enacted to illustrate what life would have been like for those forced to seek refuge there.

Several living museums celebrate the vanished patterns of the period's rural life. They use traditional livestock such as Suffolk Punch

ABOVE: Home Farm at Beamish, built in the 1780s, reflects patterns of farming life largely unchanged for centuries. Working horses, including three heavy or half-heavy breeds, are used on the fields or to pull traps as shown. Other authentic animals include rare breeds of sheep and cattle and a lively collection of pigs, hens, ducks and geese.

OPPOSITE: Women's dresses achieved their rich and stately effect through layers of linen, silk and lace, underpinned by stiffened corsets, or stays. Men's shirts were of linen with embroidered or frilled jabots at the front and ruffled cuffs, worn under elaborate waistcoats and narrow-shouldered coats. Their hats were often worn rakishly at the back of the head.

horses and regional breeds of sheep and pigs, as well as authentic farm equipment and buildings. A quarryman's house at the Museum of Welsh Life was solidly built in 1762 – the date is on the fireplace lintel – from mountain boulders and a pair of stout oak trusses to support the roof; it has a typically Welsh half-loft for the children, and its own original oak food cupboard. A smithy at the Museum of East Anglian Life at Stowmarket is still in its original, 18th-century, timber-framed building, where horse-shoeing demonstrations are regularly held. The Ryedale Folk Museum in Yorkshire has restored and displayed Stang End Cruck House to reflect the lives of John and Anne Huntley, its 18th-century owners. An inscription over the door commemorates their marriage: IH 1704, with two interlocking rings. The lingering fear of witches, typical of northeast Yorkshire, is shown by a carved witch post, designed to protect the occupants from malign influence.

The Weald and Downland Museum has several rural Georgian buildings. A barn from Hambrook has a typical 18th-century design, and granaries on mushroom-shaped stone staddles keep grain clear of damp or vermine. One granary, built in 1731, is timber-framed with brick infilling, thatched roof and original grain bins. The museum grows its own reed for thatching, keeps several types of local livestock and uses traditional methods to reconstruct and maintain buildings.

FASHION AND LEISURE

Clothes were a complicated business in Georgian times and no fashionable woman could get dressed without help. By the mid-18th century, ever-wider panniers resulted in alarming swaying as their wearers promenaded; they even had to enter rooms sideways when the fashion was at its peak. In 1742, a country lady ordering a new London outfit specified a width of 10 feet (3 m), and that was modest!

Men's clothing was similarly elaborate, although easier to move in. Breeches had a fall flap instead of a fly, and legs were flaunted in silk or cotton hose. They wore full-skirted, tight-fitting coats that reached to the knee and had narrow, unpadded shoulders, while waistcoats were richly embroidered. Wigs, worn from an early age, were the equivalent of female stays – they were uncomfortable and cumbersome articles, sweaty in hot weather and often made even heavier by pieces of lead used to achieve fashionable rolls at the side. Women's hair got higher and more elaborate through the period, despite the 'disagreeable effluvia' mentioned by a writer in 1768.

Marble Hill House, built in the 1730s for Henrietta Howard, Countess of Suffolk and mistress of George II, seems to define 18th-century aesthetic sense. Its perfect Palladian proportions epitomize the classical elegance of Georgian times, complemented by carefully landscaped grounds. Designed to provide the countess with a retreat from court life, Marble Hill became a fashionable haunt for literary and artistic figures, including Horace Walpole. Today it is a wonderful setting for those recreating the lifestyles of its aristocratic owners.

For the wealthy, the 18th century held pleasures in abundance. Ladies and gentlemen amused themselves with a wide variety of

OPPOSITE: Costumed musicians in performance at Marble Hill House. Music was one of the most popular forms of entertainment in Georgian times; family groups often played or sang together in the home, and 'celebrity' composers were household names.

Dressing the Countess of Suffolk

1 An elaborate array of perfumes, powders, puffs, combs and patches were needed in a fashionable lady's cosmetic armoury.

2 The Countess, wearing a dressing gown and an undress cap, summons her lady's maid. Assistance was essential with such complex, multi-layered dress.

3 After a linen shift and stockings, whalebone stays are laced to give shape and cleavage. The maid then adds pocket hoops for the side bustles.

4 A series of linen petticoats is followed by one of coloured silk, designed to show at the front through the open gown.

5 The final gown is slipped over the petticoats and laced together at the front, leaving a panel of silk petticoat visible beneath.

6 Pins attach an embroidered stomacher to the outer gown to hide the laces. Lastly, a cap with lace streamers is set over hair caught into a neat bun.

'Stays are a great fashion item: they give a smooth, conical torso and a great cleavage. Together with such wide panniers, you have to move slowly and much more gracefully. Slouching is not an option!'

ABOVE: Recreating music in period clothing reveals some unexpected perils. Elaborate lace cuffs or a delicate kerchief on the shoulders have to be kept clear of bow and strings, and women playing wind instruments have to accommodate a laced whalebone bodice, known as stays.

sophisticated entertainment – musical soirées, opera, dances, card parties, afternoon tea, luxurious dinners and cultured conversation. Even the process of dressing might be treated as a social occasion; visitors came and went, engaging their hostess in witty chit chat while her skilled maid added layers of garments and cosmetics. Modern interpreters have found the process to take at least 45 minutes.

Music flourished in an increasingly prosperous society, where the middle as well as upper classes enjoyed a new degree of leisure time. Recording technology did not yet exist, but singing became a highly regarded accomplishment, and the flute, oboe, violin and harpsichord were also widely played. Although we can never experience such music as freshly composed, instruments of the period, with their distinctive tonal qualities, can recapture the sound from centuries ago.

THE SPORTING LIFE

Sport, from horse racing to cockfighting and boxing – all often enlivened with gambling – played a major part in the life of wealthy young men, as spectators and participants. The opportunity for both occurred at Portchester Castle in July 2002 when the English Heritage cricket team took on a team from the National Army Museum in a re-enactment of a Georgian match. Costumes were an interesting exercise for both sides. The captains were each done up in the full rig – and very hot they were, too – but the players got away with breeches, hose and frilly shirts, which they still complained got in the way when they were trying to bowl or catch the ball. Casualties of the competitiveness of the match were the buckles and buttons used to fasten the clothes; dozens of them had to be collected from the pitch afterwards and returned with apologies to the costumiers.

'On a hot day, the wide skirts at least create a cooling breeze round the legs; but you have to be careful not to allow the skirts to fly up – we Georgian ladies wear only petticoats underneath.'

BELOW: The Georgian cricket match, played out with keen competitiveness within the walls of Portchester Castle on a very hot summer day. The players, apart from the captains, were able to strip down to shirts, breeches and hose, but the officers of the garrison, watching the game, suffered from the weight and complexity of their costumes.

ABOVE: Georgian cricket in action, complete with its two-stump wicket, absence of pads and underarm bowling techniques. The 'pitch' was small, with the sea lapping beyond the walls; one ball was lost when a particularly powerful batsman sent it right over the late Roman wall and into the Solent. The umpires were distinguished only by the canes they carried, and the authentic hired bats were shared.

Other interpreters in the audience, appropriately costumed, took full part in the proceedings; they took bets on the result, complained about cheating, kept the score by cutting notches on a stick, or simply promenaded around with fashionably haughty gaze. Authentic creams and lotions were on hand in case of injury, as well as a dish of maggots to deal with any wound resulting in putrefaction. As their owner proudly explained, 'maggots will eat anything apart from live flesh'.

The first recorded laws of the game of cricket date to 1744 – cricket has always had laws, never rules – and it is said that the brain tumour that killed Frederick, Prince of Wales, in 1751 resulted from a blow from a cricket ball. The wickets then only had two stumps, until 1775 when a leading bowler sent the ball between the stumps so often that a third was introduced. Bowling was underarm and there was no LBW law, though since pads were not worn, batsmen were understandably chary about allowing their legs to be hit. The result of this recreated match was very close, with the museum winning by three 'notches' after English Heritage had started very well and then succumbed to that enduring national malady, the middle order collapse; and despite the old-fashioned bats and the encumbering clothes, the match was played with all due competitiveness.

GEORGIAN MILITARY LIFE

The gorgeousness of civilian men's clothes during the 18th century was reflected also in military uniforms. British soldiers wore bright red coats and tricorn hats, and officers sported the gorget, a metal plate worn on their chests – the last remnant of the breastplate, at a time when body armour had virtually disappeared. Muskets had existed for decades, but an innovation now was the bayonet, a sword attached to the barrel of the musket; the first version, however, plugged directly into the barrel, preventing it being fired.

The early matchlock muskets had by now been overtaken by the flintlock, the most enduring firearm ever issued to British soldiers. Flintlock muskets were still in use in the 19th century, and are popular with re-enactors of both periods. Known as the 'Brown Bess', it was a heavy, solid gun that used pre-packaged paper cartridges with ball and powder together. It was claimed that a well-trained soldier could fire up to five rounds a minute, but it was not very accurate. As late as

ABOVE: A young rifleman of the 95th Regiment in Wellington's army at Bolsover Castle. He is firing the Baker rifle, one of the first guns to have a rifled barrel. This shot with greater accuracy, and so its owner could be deployed as a sniper with specific targets. The line infantry behind him, still equipped with muskets, use traditional tactics based on volleys of fire, from which it was hoped some shots would hit home.

'You end the day filthy, thirsty, covered in mud if it's wet … and then you remember that the real 18th-century soldiers couldn't go home to a shower and beer. It's great fun, and I've got huge respect for what those men put up with, but sometimes I'm just glad that it's not for real!'

1804, Colonel George Hanger could declare that 'a soldier must be very unfortunate indeed who shall be wounded by a common musket at 150 yards, provided his antagonist aims at him.' Officers carried flintlock pistols as secondary weapons, while Scottish pistols, or 'dags', made with an all-metal stock, allowed owners to beat their opponents to a pulp without damaging the business end of the pistol proper.

Most of the Jacobite soldiers, however, still fought with sword and shield, both of which were used offensively: the shield would punch the opponent's musket to one side while the heavy broadsword descended with fatal effect. Even in 1745 they had few guns and had to rely on the fearsomeness of their charge, fuelled by muscular speed and terrifying war cries, and urged on by the martial airs of bagpipes. So rousing were the pipes that they counted as offensive weapons; the piper James Reid found that his defence after Culloden – that he had carried no weapon – cut no ice, and he was hanged with the others.

Culloden, in 1746, was the last major pitched battle fought on British soil. The battlefield itself, now in the care of the National Trust for Scotland, contains the mass graves of Scottish clansmen, still visible today. It also has displays and interpretations of the battle, which is regularly recreated by re-enactment groups with full historical accuracy. The slaughter of the Jacobite army, a mere 5000 men arrayed against the Duke of Cumberland's better equipped and better rested

Loading and firing a flintlock musket

1 The paper cartridge, with its charge of black powder and a ball, had to be bitten open before it was used. This practice caused soldiers to develop a raging thirst during combat.

2 The firing pan is primed with a small amount of black powder. This will later be sparked by the flint, causing a 'flash in the pan' that in turn ignites the rest of the charge.

3 The remaining powder and the ball, together with the cartridge paper, are rammed down the barrel with the side of the hand. The musket must be kept carefully away from the face.

4 Pulling the trigger releases the flint, causing a spark to ignite powder in the pan, followed by the rest of the charge. Soldiers were engulfed in smoke as they discharged the weapon.

force of 9000-odd, took less than an hour, watched by camp followers on both sides. Scottish civilians suffered greatly in the aftermath – villages were burned and crofters evicted in an 18th-century outbreak of ethnic cleansing. Culloden heralded the end, not only of Jacobite political aspirations but also of feudal life in the Scottish Highlands.

The battles of the Peninsular Wars, in which British, Portuguese and rebelling Spanish troops fought against Napoleon's mighty armies, give re-enactors the chance to recreate action on a European scale. It was a bloody conflict, fought over harsh terrain and combining cavalry charges and sabres with guns and cannon, all capable of inflicting immense damage. Letters home carry graphic accounts from those who survived the terrifying battles, such as the young Edward Freer's description of Badajoz in 1812: 'Our Regt. [the 43rd] have suffered most severely in the storm, having lost Eighteen Officers killed or

BELOW: A wounded soldier from a recreated engagement in the Peninsular Wars is helped from the battlefield at Kirby Hall, Northamptonshire. This was a particularly bloody campaign and wounds were severe. William Freer, injured at Badajoz in April 1814, wrote to his father that 'Thank God we are both doing as well as the nature of our wounds can possibly admit of. My right arm was amputated having had a Musquet Shot which shattered it above the Elbow. I also had a slug in my backside which worked out the other night … it is healing up.'

wounded and three hundred and forty men, amongst the former our Colonel was killed…. We were up on the Breach for near an hour and half exposed to a most tremendous fire of musketry, hand grenades, shells, fire Balls and large stones which they threw down upon us from the Ramparts.' He was killed, aged 20, the following year.

The Georgian period was in many ways a time of contradictions – violent and dangerous, cultured and refined. For the rich, it was an age of plenty, with feasts and extravagant drinking a feature of upper-class life. Food was plentiful for the wealthy, and often indulged in to excess; modern re-enactors are generally more restrained. William Pitt regularly drank two bottles of port at a sitting, and suffered painfully from gout as a consequence. Art, architecture, literature and music flourished for the 18th-century elite, and new discoveries in science began to transform people's understanding of the world. Yet poverty, sickness, brutality and war were still endemic, the lot of most of the population, whether in country or town. Contrasts between rich and poor seem as great as ever in the 18th century; but the broadening of Georgian society and the growth in education and knowledge saw the first stirrings of the freedoms and wider opportunities available today.

ABOVE: Young drummer boys often participate in re-enacted army parades, such as this one at Kirby Hall, Northamptonshire, although older, stronger boys would have been used in combat. Drummers were paid more than ordinary soldiers: 1s 3d a day in the Napoleonic Wars as opposed to 1s, reflecting their important role.

RIGHT: A roughly contemporary sketch of the battle of Waterloo, made in 1815 by Captain Alexander Thomson and Lieutenant Francis Yarde Gilbert, and now in the National Archives. In days before photographs and television reports, such documents were the only way in which those not at the scene could get a sense of what had occurred.

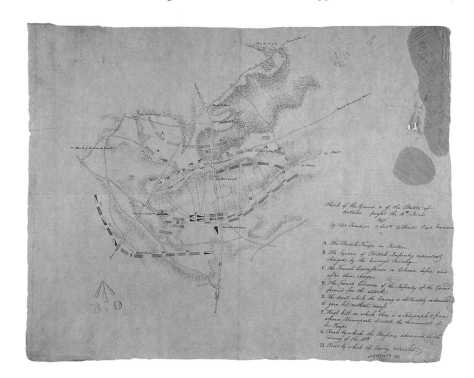

QUEEN VICTORIA REIGNED FOR MORE THAN 60 YEARS, PRESIDING OVER RAPID CHANGES THAT SHAPED OUR MODERN WORLD. ADVANCES IN INDUSTRY, ENGINEERING, SCIENCE, MEDICINE AND COMMUNICATIONS WERE COMPLEMENTED BY SOCIAL REFORMS, BUT GRINDING RURAL POVERTY

THE VICTORIAN AGE

AND GRIM URBAN SLUMS REMAINED. IT WAS AN AGE OF MATERIAL EXTREMES, BUT ALSO ONE IN WHICH CERTAINTIES WERE ERODED: DISCOVERIES IN SCIENCE CHALLENGED RELIGIOUS FAITH, MANY VIEWED RAILWAYS WITH ALARM, AND URBAN SPRAWL BEGAN TO CONSUME THE 'GREEN AND PLEASANT LAND'. DEPENDENT ON TECHNOLOGY YET WARY OF ITS CONSEQUENCES, VICTORIAN PEOPLE IN SOME WAYS SEEM NOT SO DISTANT FROM OURSELVES.

7

Approaching Victorian times

WE ARE ALL FAMILIAR with images of the Victorian world – sometimes sanitized, sometimes grotesque. The novels of Charles Dickens (and their film incarnations) illustrate urban poverty, and tourists flock to the streets where Jack the Ripper committed his real crimes – as well as to the fictional address in London's Baker Street where Sherlock Holmes solved some of the great imaginary crimes of the day. Long gone are the images of rural life in Thomas Hardy's novels, augmented by chocolate-box pictures of idyllic villages. Yet many of our lasting Christmas rituals, from the trees introduced by Prince Albert to the sending of greetings cards, were innovations of the Victorian age.

Its impact on our own era has been immense – a physical as well as a cultural legacy that is still all around us today. Many public buildings such as libraries, town halls and museums, churches and chapels, schools and hospitals, industrial mills and transport networks, even the first suburbs, were built in the 19th century. Documentary evidence for the period is abundant, including newspaper archives, census returns, official records of birth, marriage and death, records of crime and convicts, records of service in the armed forces, family archives and photographs. These last allow us to see for the first time what people really looked like and how they dressed.

The 19th century is in part defined by these new technologies. Photographs reveal real people – not just the great and good, although Victoria was the first British monarch to be photographed and even filmed in her old age. Inmates of workhouses, children on the street and in the first elementary schools, church outings and harvests, criminals and public officials, the diverse populations of servants' halls – all are recorded for posterity. We can even hear the voices of the past. Prime Minister Gladstone's voice can be heard on a very early phonograph, recorded at the request of Thomas Edison in the 1880s. He sounds just as orotund and stately as his photograph portrays him, but his accent shows clear traces of his northern origins – again a challenge to preconceptions which shape our views even of the more recent people of the past.

It was a century of transition, full of contradictions and contrasts, which is not always easy to understand. Early technology may appear to bring Victorians closer to us than other people of the past, but their lifestyles and attitudes are in some aspects very different. In exploring living museums of the Victorian era and recreating 19th-century ways of life, we are still looking from outside at a vanished age.

Visiting Victorian sites

BELOW LEFT: The 'Steam Elephant', a standard gauge steam locomotive, was designed for industrial use by William Chapman and John Buddle in 1815. It vanished in the 1840s, but was recreated by Beamish researchers from an oil painting and the account book of its construction. The magnificent boiler follows the principles of the original, modified to accommodate modern health and safety rules.

BELOW RIGHT: Today, the 'Steam Elephant' pulls carriages and gives rides to visitors at Beamish – a far cry from the original's use in collieries of the northeast. Interpreters in authentic costume here carry out the regular maintenance needed to keep the full-size replica looking at its best.

IT IS DIFFICULT NOT TO VISIT VICTORIAN SITES – they are all around us, from museums and hospitals, town halls and railway stations, to the houses in which millions of us still live. Some, like sewers, are under our feet and in the infrastructures of our homes: the engineering achievements, both great and small, that gradually improved public health and daily comfort. The 19th century saw engineering as a force to improve people's lives, encouraging the talents of visionaries such as Isambard Kingdom Brunel. Though its improvements took time to filter down, this age saw the beginnings of easier travel, more productive industry and better ways of life.

ENGINEERING AND INDUSTRY

The achievements of Brunel, the towering genius of Victorian engineering, have lasted to this day. The last of his constructions that he actually saw come to fruition was the Royal Albert Bridge over the River Tamar at Saltash. It was opened in 1859 by the Prince Consort in the presence of a gravely ill Brunel, who was carried across it during the opening ceremony but died shortly afterwards. The bridge – highly innovative in its day and still very impressive – carries today's

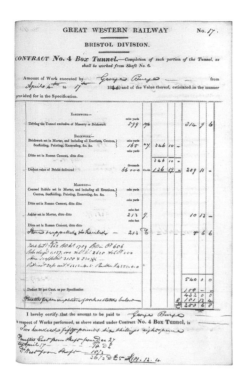

ABOVE: The detailed accounts of projects such as Brunel's Box Hill Tunnel illustrate the cost of his engineering achievements, and the confidence of the society that funded them. This account from the National Archives reveals expenditure on labour and materials during 4–17 April 1840.

'It's great to take a ride behind a real steam locomotive, with all that chugging and the smell of the smoke, but I'm not sure I'd want to have to go on a very long journey with those hard wooden seats.'

rail traffic over the Tamar to Cornwall. The trains like as not start at another of Brunel's splendid edifices, Paddington Station, recently restored to highlight the grandeur of the conception and delicacy of the decoration; the great roof arch alone is an engineering miracle. The Clifton Suspension Bridge in Bristol was another of his designs, although it was not built until after his death. Brunel was also responsible for the first iron ships and thousands of miles of railway.

We take for granted much of this railway boom, providing as it does the continuing infrastructure of our lives. Millions of passengers pass through the great railway stations daily, oblivious to the startling innovation such buildings represent: the train shed at St Pancras Station in London was the widest structure in the world when it opened. The railways themselves, as they extended their reach into ever more challenging territory, were faced with new and increasingly difficult problems. Their ingenious solutions have left us with some truly spectacular monuments – sensations such as Brunel's 1841 Box Tunnel on the Great Western Railway, which took five years to build and was an unheard-of 3 km (2 miles) in length, and the Ribblehead Viaduct on the Settle–Carlisle line, with its 24 arches, built in the 1870s and one of 21 viaducts on this most scenic of railways. The station at Ribblehead now has a visitor centre dedicated to the Settle–Carlisle line, which was re-opened in December 2000.

There were scores of small railway companies operating local services, many of which have found a new life as heritage railways for local travellers and tourists. The Keighley and Worth Valley Railway in Yorkshire, built by local mill owners in 1867, was re-opened six years after it closed in 1962 by a preservation society which has owned and run it ever since. It operates weekday morning diesels for locals, plus daily steam train services for tourists in summer and on public holidays, stopping at historic stations such as Haworth, home of the Brontës, and Oakworth, setting for the film *The Railway Children*. The Lake District's Ravenglass and Eskdale Railway advertises itself as the 'most beautiful train journey in England', while Wales has the Llangollen Railway, the Brecon Mountain Railway and the Rheilffordd Ffestiniog Railway, the oldest independent railway company in the world and still operating amidst the spectacular scenery of Snowdonia. These are over 150 heritage railways across Britain, offering the thrill of sitting behind a whistling, chugging steam locomotive and enjoying the unique tang of coal-fired smoke.

hold the numbers that are daily dying of cholera. The parish authorities have therefore resorted to the old custom of placing the surplus bodies in the vaults of the parish church. On Sunday last 14 bodies were removed for burial but twenty minutes before morning service. And throughout this week there have been daily from four & ten bodies all deceased of cholera lying under the church awaiting burial. I feel that this practice must be most injurious to the health of the congregation if not most dangerous. Two of our congregation have already died. I have myself suffered most severely, having been sick last Sunday night. But, through the mercy of God, I am now I trust recovering.

If your Lordship should

LEFT: Cholera was a scourge of 19th-century cities; over 40,000 people died in the great epidemics of 1849 and 1854. This letter in the National Archives, from another outbreak in 1866, is by the vicar of St George in the East, London. He strongly warns against the practice of placing bodies of cholera victims in the church vaults before burial, as many of his congregation had died as a result of exposure to bodies that were still infectious.

Traditional railway routes are augmented by railway history collections held by living museums such as Amberley Working Museum in West Sussex, where the important collection of narrow-gauge railway equipment is made real by trips on a narrow-gauge railway itself.

Pumping stations may seem unlikely visitor attractions, yet their combination of engineering skill with exuberant Victorian decoration reflects the spirit of the age. In Nottinghamshire, the Papplewick water pumping station, built in 1884, is open to the public. The ornate floral design of its ironwork complements the two working beam pumping engines, thought to be the last built by the famous James Watt & Co, at a cost of £5525 each including installation.

Even sewers have their splendour. The magnificent Crossness pumping station, built by the great Victorian engineer Sir Joseph Bazalgette, is now a Grade I listed building, with four original pumping engines and some of London's finest Victorian ironwork. A walk along Victoria Embankment on the north side of the Thames traces part of Bazalgette's brilliant scheme to channel waste into his new sewers, built after terrible cholera outbreaks in 1849 and 1854.

OPPOSITE: The interior of a sawmill from Ty'n Rhos, Llanddewi-Brefi, Ceredigion, built in 1892 and re-erected in 1994 at the Museum of Welsh Life. A sawmill had been established there in 1868, but by 1892 a water-powered circular saw had become available through new technology, and this building was erected to house it. The family who owned the business were highly regarded as makers of quality joinery work, furniture, carts and wagons.

ABOVE: Victorian metalworking machinery is stored in the principal ground floor room of 94 Vyse Street in the Birmingham Jewellery Quarter. The house was built as a residence around 1860, and domestic features such as fireplace and cornice still remain, but, like many surrounding houses, it has long since been colonized for industrial use.

The buildings of the Birmingham Jewellery Quarter, one of Britain's most important industrial heritage sites, are still used for their original purpose. Many retain their original layout and use small machines of 18th- or 19th-century origin – still the best tools for the job. The Quarter's dense concentration of converted houses and specialist buildings, all associated with jewellery and metalworking, is probably unique; the more remarkable as it is very much a living, working community. Jewellers still work at battered old 'peg benches' in the first-floor workshop at Alabaster & Wilson, and the second-floor press room, with its fly presses and their attachments, is in use at 94 Vyse Street. The Museum of the Jewellery Quarter is situated in buildings once occupied by Smith & Pepper, makers of gold jewellery. All the authentic tools and machinery involved in jewellery-making are on view and there are regular demonstrations and guided tours.

VICTORIAN HOUSES AND HOMES

Millions of us still live in houses built by the Victorians, ranging in size from splendid townhouses, now mostly divided into flats, to rows of small terraces. A recent *cause célèbre* was the National Trust's purchase of the gloriously Gothic Tyntesfield, an enormous and ornate house built in the 1860s for the guano magnate William Gibbs. When it opens to the public, it will be a microcosm of grand Victorian style.

The extraordinary Cragside in Northumberland reveals many Victorian enthusiasms and idiosyncrasies. Built in the 1880s for the lawyer turned industrialist Lord Armstrong, it was designed with hot and cold running water, central heating, fire alarms, telephones, a passenger lift and the first hydroelectric lighting system in the world. Cragside's exuberantly decorated dining room is one of the finest Victorian domestic rooms in Britain, with many original contents.

In London, Leighton House was the sumptuous home of the artist Frederic, Lord Leighton. His magnificent studio lies at the heart of the house, with great north windows and a gilded dome and apse, while the Arab Hall has glorious tiles and a fountain playing in the middle of the floor.

Brodsworth Hall in Yorkshire is now a paradigm of modern conservation techniques that allow for wear and tear. It is a place with lots of stories to tell, a place where it sometimes seems possible almost to touch the real people who lived there. The so-called Lathe Room is stuffed with accumulated junk – old tennis racquets in their wooden presses, a wartime gas mask, arrays of tools and moth-eaten stuffed birds in glass cases, all now carefully conserved. More objects are constantly coming to light. One recent discovery in an outhouse was a Berthon boat, a collapsible dinghy invented in the late 19th century. The family left the original kitchen for a more modern one in the 1920s. They just shut the door on the old one, which is now a time capsule of a Victorian kitchen in a great house, staffed with servants.

Down House in north Kent was the home of Charles Darwin, the greatest iconoclast of the Victorian age. Here Darwin wrote *On the Origin of Species by Natural Selection*, shaking the foundations of Victorian society by proposing an alternative to the biblical view of human origins. Down House and its grounds are being restored to how they were when he lived there. Darwin's study is as it was when he worked in it, with papers and books, multi-shelf files and the chair in which he wrote on a cloth-covered board balanced across the arms. The authentic contents of the house not only reflect his scientific scholarship but also give evidence of his family life, including his grief for his daughter, Annie, who died tragically young.

ABOVE: The Drawing Room at Brodsworth Hall is a monument to the high Victorian love of elaborate decoration, complete with Corinthian columns, ornate furniture and sparkling chandeliers. Brodsworth also reflects the modern preference for displaying grand houses of the past complete with the evidence of their change and decay.

OPPOSITE: Charles Darwin's study at Down House is much as it was when the great man lived, studied and wrote there. Visitors come to explore the house and grounds today in homage to one of the great geniuses of the age, whose discoveries revolutionized scientific understanding.

Perhaps the greatest Victorian 'home' is Osborne House on the Isle of Wight, built for Queen Victoria and Prince Albert as a family home and refuge from the cares of state. The pomp and splendour of the recently restored Durbar Room contrast with intimate and comfortable family rooms, allowing visitors to imagine a real family growing up here. Human touches within the grandeur include the Prince Consort's bath and shower, novelties in the mid-19th century, complemented by those fitted for the queen in her dressing room; the lift, manually operated from the basement, added in 1893 to give the ageing queen easier access to her first-floor suite of rooms; the nursery suite; and the small Horn Room, where Victoria's birthday table was sometimes set out. Life below stairs is glimpsed in table deckers' rooms under the dining room, with cupboards – painted blue to discourage flies – for chinaware and lead-lined sinks for washing glassware.

ABOVE: The rear façade of Osborne House on the Isle of Wight, designed and built in the Italianate style by Prince Albert and Thomas Cubitt. Osborne was intended to be a country home for the royal family, and it enjoyed wonderful views over the grounds and the Solent beyond. Victoria called Osborne her 'island paradise', and she died here on 22 January 1901, after 64 years on the throne.

'*Nobody caught cold or smelt paint, and it was a most amusing event, the coming here. Everything in the house is quite new, and the dining room looked very handsome. The windows, lighted by the brilliant lamps in the room, must have been seen far out at sea. After dinner we rose to drink the Queen's and Prince's health as a house-warming … And truly entering a new house, a new palace, is a solemn thing to do.*'

LADY LYTTLETON, ON THE DAY WHEN THE ROYAL FAMILY MOVED INTO THEIR NEW APARTMENTS IN THE PAVILION AT OSBORNE IN 1846

GUNS AND GUNBOATS

In the 19th century Britannia really did rule the waves, and the dockyards at Portsmouth and Chatham adapted to the new age of steam. Visitors stepping aboard HMS *Warrior* at Portsmouth catch an intimate glimpse of life on board the world's first iron-hulled armoured warship, powered by steam as well as sail. Built in 1860, the *Warrior* was the most formidable warship the world had ever seen. Today it looks as it did on its first commission in 1861–4, as if the crew had just gone ashore and left everything ready for inspection.

At Chatham, new engineering skills and technology designed covered slips, sloping down to the river where most ships were built. These slips reflect rapid technological change: the first slip roof is of timber, the next three largely of cast iron, and the fifth, No. 7 Slip, dating from 1855, has a cast- and wrought-iron frame and a modern metal trussed roof. Also at Chatham is HMS *Gannet*, a Victorian warship built in 1878, which saw action all over the world; it is now being returned to the shape and condition it enjoyed in 1886.

Other nations were also developing faster, steam-driven ships, independent of wind and tide, which presented a renewed threat to England's south coast. Two massive wings were added to Hurst Castle in the 1860s and 1870s, and Portsmouth's defences were strengthened by the Gosport Advanced Line (five forts built across the Gosport peninsula). Fort Brockhurst is one of these, its strategic polygonal shape designed to accommodate more guns in more flexible positions.

RIGHT: The Victorian age was a time of relative domestic peace, but an expanding empire led to military and naval actions overseas. The armed forces became a focus of patriotic pride; the 1st Battalion of the Middlesex Regiment, for example, obtained their nickname of the 'Diehards' from an engagement in the Peninsular Wars. Here the battalion displays the uniform and equipment of the 1880s: Home Service review order dress, spiked helmets (worn until the start of World War I) and Martini Henry rifles.

Recreating the past

THE REALITY OF LIVING IN A LATE VICTORIAN HOUSE was recreated in a recent television programme, *The 1900 House*. The Bowlers family of six lived for three months in a London house that had been returned to its 1900 condition; no central heating, electric light or modern plumbing and only a coal-fired range for cooking and hot water. The shock was substantial: all housework was done by hand, and chores that today take minutes lasted all day. Laundry was hard physical labour, involving the pounding of clothes with a wooden 'dolly', and keeping fires burning was constant, dirty work. There was no shampoo, shaving was with a cut-throat razor, the toilet was outside and a jug and basin replaced plumbed washbasins. Despite the family's genuine enthusiasm and interest, the children at least were very keen to return to today's more comfortable world.

LIVING IN VICTORIAN TOWNS

Several living museums of this period illustrate working communities, both in countryside and towns. Many of the latter were centred on

BELOW: Bates & Hunt, the chemist's shop at Blists Hill, is staffed, fitted out and stocked as in Victorian times, when it offered a range of services to this small industrial town. It dispensed medicines and sold herbal remedies, patent medicines and toiletries as well as household goods. The shop was also the place to come for advice and help if the doctor's fee could not be afforded.

RIGHT AND BELOW: Inside and outside views of the squatter's cottage at Blists Hill, reconstructed there in 1978. In 1861 it was inhabited by a cobbler, his wife, three strapping coalminer sons, two daughters who were iron ore pickers, a 5-year-old son and a 10-year-old visitor – nine occupants packed into a tiny space. All had to be catered for over the simple kitchen range. Landowners often tacitly approved of such roughly-built cottages, in which their workers often lived. They charged no rent, but instead levied an annual 'fine' for encroachment.

specific industries, such as dockyards or mill towns, pit villages or the railway towns of Swindon or Crewe. Blists Hill, one of the Ironbridge Gorge museums, recreates a late Victorian town near Coalbrookdale ironworks, a major industrial centre. Interpreters in costume work in shops and houses, demonstrating the daily routines of 150 years ago.

The first stop at Blists Hill is the recreated bank of Vickers, Son & Pritchard, 19th-century Shropshire bankers later bought out by Lloyds. Modern money can be exchanged there for tokens to spend in the town's shops. In the chemist's, medical and household items are on sale, such as carbolic soap with its all-pervading smell, while the sweetshop entices with old-fashioned sherbets and liquorice. And then there are the butcher, the baker, the candlestick-maker … Home-baked bread is on sale at Farryner's, the baker's, and pork pies at the butcher's shop. In its original position on a steep hill in Ironbridge, the butcher's had a cellar living room used by the husband, wife, three sons and a servant girl. Candles were vital for homes and industries, and Blists Hill candle factory hangs finished ones from the ceiling, a traditional practice preventing them from being eaten by rats.

Also on show in this Victorian town are the shops and workshops of the tradesmen – the plumber and tinsmith, the plasterer and cobbler, the printer, the harness-maker, the carpenter and the small jobbing foundry and wrought ironworks. The drapers and milliners was one of the few businesses that women could set up; their domestic work can also be glimpsed in the squatter cottage, reconstructed here in 1978. Blists Hill also has a school, dating from 1881, and a surgery, where a visiting doctor dispensed medicines and performed minor operations, in return – before the NHS – for payment in cash or kind.

The river banks of the Doon Valley, Ayrshire, reveal the layers of coal, clay, limestone and blackband ironstone that made the region an industrial heartland. Dunaskin Open Air Museum celebrates the legacy of that industry, which started with ironworks in the 1840s and moved on to coal mining and a brickworks in the 20th century. Among the surviving buildings are the Grade A-listed Blowing Engine House, the only one left in Europe from this period, with elaborate Italianate detailing. Cottages on Chapel Row show typical workers' housing and one, restored to its 1914 condition, is open to visitors. Dunaskin owns an impressive collection of vintage steam locomotives and rolling stock, and the museum runs regular Steam Days.

ABOVE: The Black Country Living Museum at Dudley is built at a site where there were once over 40 mine shafts. One has been opened to visitors, headed by the wooden pit frame. A steam-powered engine, with a single cylinder outside drum, winds the cage up and down the shaft, 30m in depth.

LEFT: The Black Country Living Museum is built around two original branches of the Birmingham canal system, used to link lime kilns to the region's main transport routes. In the foreground are replica working barges that once carried wood, coal and glass; behind is the reconstructed Anchor Forge, with its towering chimney, reflecting the area's metalworking traditions. The forge hammer and furnace were brought from Cradley Heath, also in the West Midlands, while the forge building itself originally stood in West Bromwich.

RIGHT: The Boat Dock at the Black Country Living Museum is fully equipped to build and repair canal boats. It is typical of many such docks in the Black Country, and essential to the canal system that once maintained Britain's industrial infrastructure.

ABOVE: A pit pony at Beamish Open Air Museum is used to pull small wagons, a reminder of the jobs done by its predecessors, including hauling tubs of coal to the surface in the local collieries. Animals had important roles in both farming and industry until very recently.

Dunaskin is peopled, too, with authentic photographs showing individuals and groups of workers throughout the site's history. One impressively early photograph shows a furnace crew in 1850, complete with a row of young boys whose job it was to make the 'pig beds' into which the molten iron was poured.

The Black Country Living History Museum at Dudley in the West Midlands focuses on the lifestyles, skills and enterprises of the people of what was once the industrial heart of Britain. The mining area has the only working full-scale replica of the world's first steam engine, the Newcomen Engine of 1712, as well as a spectacular underground mining display complete with creaking pit props and rock falls, and an ironworks where all sorts of crafts are demonstrated. The village has a school, pub and shops, together with the back-to-back houses of the 1850s and workers' cottages from the late 18th century. The main focus is on the canal, built in the 18th century but in use through the 19th and into the early 20th century. It surrounds the village on three sides and forms part of the Birmingham canal system. Two arms lead to old lime kilns and a functioning boatdock, and trips can be taken through the Dudley Tunnel, 2884 m (3154 yds) long and connecting to a network of caverns and canal branches serving limestone mines. Boats were originally 'legged' through the tunnel by men who lay on their backs and pushed the boat along with their feet braced against the roof and walls. This method was tried again when the tunnel opened to visitors in the 1970s; it was very hard work! Boats making the trip now use electricity, the only other method possible because of the lack of ventilation in the tunnel.

The North of England Open Air Museum at Beamish in County Durham illustrates daily working life in northeast England at two dates that straddle the Victorian period; they thus encompass the full range of how life developed and changed. The earlier period concentrates on the lifestyle of a yeoman farming family at Pockerley Manor in 1825, together with a railway reconstructed to allow visitors to experience the early days of steam. Replica, unsprung 1825 railway carriages are pulled either by a replica of George Stephenson's 'Locomotion No. 1' (the original of which headed the first public, passenger-carrying steam train in the world on the Stockton & Darlington Railway in 1825), or by the new, full-size, working replica of the once-lost 'Steam Elephant' (page 152). The museum also has the magnificent Hetton Locomotive, built by Stephenson in 1822 and said to be the third oldest surviving railway engine in the world.

OPPOSITE: The blacksmith at Beamish, a modern exponent of the crafts that sustained village and small community life. He was a skilled ironworker who produced many of the items necessary for farming communities, such as farm implements and the rims of wheels, as well as keeping working horses well-shod and efficient.

BELOW: At Blists Hill the tinsmith worked in sheet metal, including zinc, copper and tinplate, to make food and cooking utensils, among them 'snap' (lunch) boxes for miners. The collection of tools and equipment around him comes from the workshops of H. Topp, tinsmiths near Coventry for three generations.

The later period centres on 1913, the year before World War I put an irrevocable end to traditional Victorian and Edwardian ways of life. The recreated town features a typical street of the period, complete with bank, solicitor's office, dentist's surgery, newspaper office, printing works, sweet shop, garage, livery stables and a public house, as well as other houses and shops. The colliery village has a terrace of miners' cottages –where bread-baking and mat-making are regularly demonstrated – a local school and chapel. The drift mine is open to visitors; they can also admire the complete machinery of the pit-head, including a steam winding engine that works but no longer raises and lowers cages into the mine. The working home farm is stocked with traditional breeds of livestock and poultry, and the farm kitchen offers a warm welcome.

The whole ethos of Beamish is centred on getting close to real life in a specific time and place. It is staffed by interpreters in period costume who carry out traditional tasks using authentic techniques and materials. Beamish recreates a whole environment – work, home life, schooling and leisure – as it would have been experienced by those actually living there in 1825 and 1913. All kinds of living history events are on offer, from May Day festivities in the colliery village to a costumed school sports day, a Harvest Home supper and ploughing matches, as well as practical crafts and activities such as lace-making.

LIFE IN THE COUNTRYSIDE

In little over 100 years, Britain's traditional, rural way of life has vanished into the distant past. So great was the transformation during the 20th century that a countryman living 150 years ago would have felt more in tune with his predecessors of several centuries ago than with those who farm the land today. It is easy to feel nostalgia for a lost golden age, but the realities of Victorian country life were often harsh. The landscape itself may prove deceptive: picturesque, highly renovated cottages owned by wealthy families today belie their earlier existence as run-down hovels of landless labourers – frequently damp, dark and infested with fleas and rats.

As rural Britain changed in the 20th century, many historic buildings fell prey to developers and road-builders. Open-air museums, such as the Weald and Downland Museum near Chichester in Sussex and the Chiltern Open Air Museum in Buckinghamshire, have helped to preserve a living heritage by rescuing and re-erecting

'Under the spreading chestnut tree
The village smithy stands;
The smith, a mighty man is he,
With large and sinewy hands;
And the muscles of his brawny arms
Are strong as iron bands.'

HENRY WADSWORTH LONGFELLOW,
THE VILLAGE BLACKSMITH

vernacular buildings in their regions. The Chiltern Open Air Museum has 19th-century cart sheds and a cattle shelter, a mission room and an assembly shop for making Windsor chairs. It also has a forge, built about 1860 and worked by members of the same family until 1926.

For centuries the blacksmith was one of the most important craftsmen in the rural community, making and repairing farm implements and tools as well as shoeing horses and fitting metal tyres on the wooden wheels of carts. At Ryedale Folk Museum in Yorkshire a recreated smithy is manned by volunteers, and demonstrations of the blacksmith's art are also carried out at the Museum of East Anglian Life at Stowmarket in Suffolk. The smithy here originally came from Grundisburgh and was in regular use until 1968 when the last smith, Frederick Crapnell, retired (aged 86!) after taking over the smithy in 1913. The museum also has working steam-driven agricultural engines (including the magnificent Empress) used for ploughing and threshing, as well as for powering saws and other farm machinery. At Amberley Working Museum in West Sussex, a variety of craftspeople, including a blacksmith, a potter, and makers of brooms, walking sticks and clay pipes, ply their trade and sell their traditional produce.

Another evocative feature of Victorian life is the recreation at the Museum of East Anglian Life of a small rural house, with its parlour, or 'best room', and its kitchen with solid fuel range and washing copper. The mangle and flat irons recall the heavy work of washdays before automatic washing machines and electric irons, all made much worse if it was a wet or windless day and the washing failed to dry. This house, of course, lacked electricity or gas, like many others well into the 20th century, and the privy was an earth closet outside with its spiders, smells and eeriness in the dark and the winter – hence the convenient chamber pot in the bedroom. Ryedale, too, has a cottage reconstructed as it would have been at the end of the 19th century, complete with a washhouse and dairy that were used for a range of jobs. Pig-killing, bacon-salting and separating honey were all done in these rooms, and the copper built into the corner could be used for boiling puddings and scalding poultry as well as washing clothes.

Shops at these living museums are a reminder of life before our pre-packed age. Salt came in long, thick bars, to be carved up into slices; butter was shaped into saleable quantities using wooden butter pats. Slabs of soap were cut off from long bars, and customers brought their own bottles and jugs for liquid goods such as vinegar and milk.

ABOVE: Saddleback pigs, taller than their keepers when they stand on their hind legs, are a feature of Beamish's Home Farm. They are one of the regional breeds to be found here, along with Teeswater sheep, Shorthorn cattle – descendants of the Durham ox – and many poultry varieties. The combined pig sty and hen house was built in the 19th century.

BELOW: In the 19th century Harome Cottage, now rebuilt near its original site at the Ryedale Folk Museum, was the home of Mr and Mrs Taylor who ran the village school. Its garden is planted with flowers and vegetables typical of cottage gardens. Rare plant varieties, such as fir apple potatoes, the Hutton Wonder pea and bi-coloured runner beans, underpinned the domestic rural economy.

Living museums often draw upon historic sites and structures to provide a more accurate glimpse into an alien world. Gressenhall Museum of Rural Life in Norfolk, for example, is housed in a converted workhouse; its grim regime was once a source of dread for the local community, and in 1897 a disabled man from Dereham committed suicide rather than be admitted there. Living close to the land was an uncertain condition, exposed to the vagaries of the natural and economic climate. For most of the 19th century a failed harvest meant hunger, poverty and unemployment were always round the corner, and the village was the focus of a much more localized world.

Gressenhall's Union Farm features many breeds native to the region, including Large Black pigs, Norfolk Horn sheep, Red Poll cattle and the Suffolk Punch horses that are regularly to be seen at work in the fields. The rural setting is an integral part of re-enactment at Gressenhall, providing the context that governed peoples' lives. Awareness of changing seasons was far greater, with festivals and even commercial rent days still clearly linked to the unfolding agricultural year. Entertainment was simple, traditional and homemade, and leisure time strictly limited; even after school attendance became compulsory for younger children, most continued to help their families on the land and many missed school altogether at the busiest

'The horses are so huge … and so are the pigs. And only 100 years ago these weren't the rare breeds they are today, but a regular part of a farmer's stock. It's sad to think that it took only a few decades for them to disappear from normal farming, but marvellous to work with them again here.'

RIGHT: Clydesdale heavy horses are a rare breed with origins in the north of England, so their presence at Beamish is appropriate. Essential to working farms of the Victorian period, they congregate in their splendour at Beamish's annual ploughing match. Ploughmen and horses from across the country compete, often accompanied by spectators in Victorian costume. Another competition focuses on horse dressing, when harnesses are decorated with magnificent traditional designs.

LEFT: Preparing food without modern equipment was a time-consuming process, as this busy farm kitchen at Gressenhall shows. Everything was done by hand, including plucking and gutting poultry and game, picking and peeling fruit and vegetables, and preserving food for the winter. Cooking was done over a fire in the range, and water had to be fetched in pails from the well.

ABOVE: The smock worn here by the Gressenhall shepherd is remarkable for the fine decoration and finish lavished on what was a working garment. Smocks were amazingly hard-wearing, however, and would last for several years before wearing out.

times, such as harvest. Country children, as always, made their own amuseuments – traditional games, singing and dancing, playing in the woods, fields and rivers that defined their world. Most came from large families and were expected to look after younger siblings as well as help with livestock or the endless round of domestic tasks. Re-enactors in costume recreate the events of life at Gressenhall, from lessons in the Victorian schoolroom to the often harsh experiences of pauper inmates in the workhouse. They also recreate the celebrations that strengthened the close-knit community, such as a farm picnic with authentic food and games, or a Victorian village pageant.

The brochure for the Weald and Downland Open Air Museum contains a photograph given to the museum by the step-grandaughter of a woman featured in it. She is seated in front of Poplar Cottage, a building from the mid-17th century reconstructed on the Weald and Downland site. The photograph dates from the late 19th century, when Poplar Cottage may well have been falling into disrepair. Such a glimpse into the Victorian age is uniquely tantalizing – so near and yet so far. The woman has a real, close connection to someone of the later 20th century, yet the life she led, and the whole world she knew, now seem very far away. The 'Victorians' were our grandparents and great-grandparents – but they were irrevocably of another age.

ABOVE: For today's children, here wearing Victorian costume and enjoying a picnic at Gressenhall, living history offers insights into times when school came second to the pressing needs of harvest. The chance to swish around in long skirts is fun for girls who are more used to trousers, but they can also become an encumbrance when serious work needs to be done.

LEFT: Sheep on Gressenhall's Union Farm are allowed to graze pasture in a traditional manner. Shepherds are a rarity in Britain now, but it was once a common trade, involving detailed knowledge of the flocks.

THE 20TH CENTURY IS OFTEN SAID TO HAVE BEGUN

IN 1914, WHEN THE SOCIAL STRUCTURES AND

VALUES OF THE EDWARDIAN AGE WERE SHATTERED

BY WORLD WAR I. THE DEVASTATED COUNTRY OF

1918 GAVE SOME WOMEN THE VOTE AND SAW

FURTHER SOCIAL CHANGES, BUT ITS INDUSTRIAL

THE EARLY 20TH CENTURY

MOMENTUM WAS CHALLENGED IN THE 1920S AND

'30S BY ECONOMIC DECLINE. WORLD WAR II

BROUGHT MODERN WARFARE'S DANGERS AND

HARDSHIPS TO CIVILIANS ACROSS BRITAIN, AS WELL

AS TO FIGHTING MEN. POST-WAR AUSTERITY AND

REBUILDING LASTED THROUGHOUT THE '50S, BUT

NEW STYLES OF MUSIC, THE END OF BRITAIN'S

EMPIRE AND AN INCREASING USE OF TECHNOLOGY

WERE SOON POINTING THE WAY FORWARD.

8

Approaching the 20th century

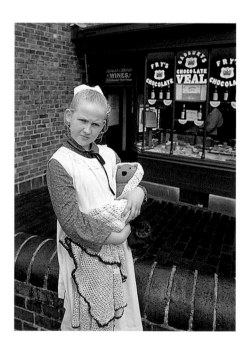

LOOKING BACK AT, and seeking to recreate, events from the early 20th century has its own particular problems. Much of the period is well within living memory, yet attitudes, expectations and patterns of life are so different that the early decades of the century seem very remote. For those living through them, the pace of change must have been bewildering, as the certainties of Edwardian Britain, shaped by the Victorian genius for technology, engineering and empire-building, were shattered in less than four years by World War I.

The Great War still casts long shadows into our present. There are men now living who as boys survived the carnage of the trenches, and bodies are still found in the makeshift graves scratched out for them. Great efforts are made to give them names, contact descendants and rebury them with full military honours; but for thousands their only memorial is still 'A soldier of the Great War. Known unto God'.

The landscape also bears the scars. The line of the Western Front in France is revealed in the white chalk subsoil, torn up by the shelling and still littering the surface. Bracken-covered humps of the British front line can be followed at Thiepval Wood under the British memorial to the battle of the Somme, where there were 1,300,000 casualties on both sides – 73,412 of them still officially 'missing'.

A generation severed from its parents' past created the new social climate of the 1920s and '30s that we now think of in clichés – flappers and tea dances, Bertie Wooster and Hercule Poirot, the glamour of cars, cocktails and foreign travel – for the rich, at least. But the reality for most was still the grinding poverty that we see reflected in images of the General Strike and the Jarrow March, underlain in the later 1930s by the threat of war yet again looming in Europe.

Over 50 years after its conclusion, World War II is still part of our everyday world. Its survivors, military and civilian, contribute to memories of the period and march on Remembrance Day in memory of lost comrades. The war still attracts makers of films and television series, from *'Allo 'Allo*, with its caricatures of the French Resistance, German military and upper-crust British airmen, to *Saving Private Ryan*, an all-too-realistic portrayal of the terrors of landing on Omaha Beach on D-Day. The period's fascination lies in the tension between this familiarity and its vast, unimaginable difference from how we live now; a huge divide exists between those who can remember World War II and those born after it. This gulf in experience, the legacy of great social and technological change, is unique to our modern age.

Visiting 20th-century sites

'The Edwardian was the last age in which a rich man could afford to build himself a new and enormous country house with a formal landscape garden, a lily pond and clipped hedges.'

JOHN BETJEMAN

BELOW: Witley Court in Worcestershire symbolizes how country houses fell out of use in the 20th century. Originally a Jacobean manor house, it was converted in the 19th century into a vast Italianate mansion in spectacular gardens, and was a centre of wealthy 19th- and early 20th century society. But new economic conditions after the Great War meant that it was never rebuilt after a disastrous fire in 1937.

THE CENTURY SAW WIDESPREAD DESTRUCTION of buildings, both from the bombings of World War II that destroyed scores of city and town centres, and changing social structures that made hundreds of grand houses expensive millstones around their owners' necks. Structures that survived from the early decades of the century include public buildings, hotels, places of work, schools and ordinary homes, from humble terraces to the urban villas of a prosperous middle class – many still used and inhabited today. Sites from the early 20th century are the most varied in history, ranging from renovated and restored buildings of the past, brought up to date for recent use, to the glories of the Edwardian age and the Art Deco of the 1930s.

AN EDWARDIAN LEGACY

The Edwardian period is only 100 years ago. But it is another world – one brought to life in the television series *The Edwardian Country House*. This recreation of the lives of the wealthy Oliff-Cooper family and their servants between 1905 and 1914 was staged at Manderston, a grand house on the Scottish borders, open to the public. It was extensively refurbished in 1905, during a decade that saw the final flowering of grand country houses, designed to provide their owners with a life of luxury and comfort, served by armies of domestics. The house has suites of spacious rooms, the only silver staircase in the world, and four terrace gardens still planted in the Edwardian style.

Under Manderston's influence, the 21st-century volunteers re-discovered the hierarchies of pre-war life. The unmarried sister Miss Anson, extremely successful in today's world, held a lowly position in the 'upstairs' family. 'Downstairs', the butler ruled with a rod of iron

over servants whose status was clearly defined; the first footman took precedence over the second, and both outranked the hall boy.

Other great Edwardian houses, either refurbished or newly built, also reflect the new century's prosperity and confidence. Sir Edwin Lutyens designed some of the finest, their gardens laid out by his favoured designer Gertrude Jekyll. The National Trust opens some of them to visitors, such as Lindisfarne Castle, a Tudor fort remodelled by Lutyens with a Jekyll garden, where opening hours reflect the tide table; or Castle Drogo, Devon, where 20th-century comfort combines with the forbidding grandeur of a faux medieval castle. Visitors may contrast the elegant drawing and dining rooms upstairs with the extensive kitchens below, and play croquet on the huge circular lawn. In Scotland, Charles Rennie Mackintosh's buildings show a different aesthetic: the Willow Tearooms in Sauchiehall Street, Glasgow, where you can take tea on reconstructed Mackintosh furniture behind a remarkable façade; Glasgow School of Art with its stupendous library; and The Hill House, built for the publisher Walter Blackie in 1902–4.

ABOVE AND RIGHT: Art Deco splendour has been triumphantly restored at Eltham Palace, where the Courtaulds built a new house on to medieval remains. The dining room doors (above) combine geometric designs with applied lacquer animals and birds. They lead into the circular entrance hall (right), with its vast glass domed roof. It is a splendid evocation of 1930s glamour, especially when adorned with interpreters in period dress.

ABOVE: The Anti-Aircraft Operations Room in the Napoleonic tunnels under Dover Castle has been partly reassembled to its appearance during World War II. The movements of enemy aircraft were charted on the illuminated screens and coordinated on the planning tables, and important information relayed through the earphones. In 1940 the evacuation of Dunkirk was masterminded from these tunnels by Admiral Ramsay, and Winston Churchill often visited them.

'A visitor to the tunnels asked about the re-enactor in World War II uniform that she'd seen in the Operations Room. I told her we didn't have anyone like that on the staff. "Have I seen a ghost, then?" she asked, and I had to admit that there have been some other sightings like hers. She went quite white.'

A PALACE OF THE 1930S

In the period between the wars, the influence of Art Deco resulted in some magnificent buildings. One of the finest is Eltham Palace in southeast London, where Stephen and Virginia Courtauld bolted a stunning contemporary house on to the remains of a medieval palace. The Courtaulds restored the Great Hall, built in the reign of Edward IV, with its splendid false hammerbeam roof, and added a home for themselves and their pet lemur, Mah-Jongg, whose centrally heated quarters are still on view. The whole house is sumptuous and rich, and has been restored as closely as possible to what it was like when the Courtaulds lived in it. A visitor's chance remark that she remembered pink leather chairs in the dining room, for example, gave an invaluable clue to restorers working from black and white photographs.

Visitors to Eltham today can marvel at the splendour of the 1930s rooms, from the magnificent vestibule and dining room to the family's bedrooms and bathrooms, juxtaposed with medieval remains. The reception rooms and the Great Hall can be hired for events, allowing people to mingle in spirit with medieval and Tudor royalty (Eltham was Henry VIII's boyhood home) and the grandees of 70 years ago.

THE SECRET TUNNELS OF WORLD WAR II

During World War II historic coastal fortifications, such as Henry VIII's castles at Portland and Pendennis, housed troops and artillery against the threat of invasion during the battle of Britain. The strategic strength of Dover Castle's location came into its own again in 1940, when tunnels burrowed into the chalk cliffs in Napoleonic times provided operations rooms for the Dover Command, Coastal Artillery and Anti-Aircraft activities. The tunnels also provided the command post for Admiral Ramsay during the evacuation of Dunkirk. The reconstructed rooms, with their 'state of the art' radio equipment, can still be seen, together occasionally with the fleeting ghosts of some of those who operated them – several sightings have been reported.

The tunnels now include recreations of the barracks and field hospital for the wounded that they contained during World War II. Uncomfortable-looking canvas beds combine with cooking smells and the groans of a wounded man, as surgeons struggle to operate while lights flicker and bombs crash outside. The operating theatre is almost too bloodily authentic; but it is all highly evocative of those dark days when the first invasion since 1066 was a very real possibility.

Recreating the past

RE-ENACTORS OF THE EARLY 20TH CENTURY have a wide choice of themes, from military and support roles in the World Wars to the lifestyles of the rich in Edwardian times and between the wars. They can also open an imaginative window into the less glamorous lives of our grandparents and great-grandparents, in conditions little different from the 19th century. Lots of authentic costume and equipment is available, but the quantity of first-hand witnesses and accounts means that re-enactors have to be careful in tackling such a recent past.

LIVING MEMORY AND LIVING MUSEUMS

Living museums bring to life for all ages the ordinary places where people lived and worked. The North of England Open Air Museum at Beamish recreates a cobbled 1913 street with a branch of Barclays Bank, a dentist, a solicitor's office, a printer's workshop, a pub, a co-operative store, a sweetshop and electric trams, all featuring interpreters in authentic costume. The recreated colliery village has its board school, its Methodist chapel and pit cottages, their gardens stocked with poultry, rabbits and pigeons. Visitors can go down the mine and conjure up miners of the past, who emerged from a hard day's work and tramped home covered in black coal dust; pithead baths were not installed in many places until much later. Beamish offers lots of occasions that would have been enjoyed by the people who lived in its 1913 town, such as morris dancing and brass band concerts; and it holds an Empire weekend when the town is festooned with flags and bunting – a celebration of the innocent patriotism that took such a drubbing in World War I.

The huge contrast between the lives of the owners of Manderston and Eltham and those of ordinary people at Beamish is also pointed up at the Black Country Living Museum, near Dudley in the West Midlands. Here the Racecourse Colliery is shown as it would have been in 1910, together with one-up one-down cottages recreated according to a photograph of *c*.1900. These are equipped with a cast-iron pump, used to draw rainwater collected from the roof, and the water boiler with the 'posser', the manual forerunner to the washing machine. The school there is much as it was when it was improved in 1912; today's children go there to dress up in the clothes of the time, sit on hard wooden benches and experience the schooldays of the past.

The museum has many shops, including Gregory's Store, which sold virtually everything needed by the community: meat and dairy

BELOW: Inside a back-to-back house from a recreation of 1920s life at the Black Country Living Museum. The kitchen hearth was a focal point in an era before central heating, providing warmth, light, hot water for cooking and washing and a good spot to dry and air clothes. In the days before pithead baths – as late as the 1950s in some parts of the country – miners would have washed away the coal dust in a tin bath in front of a fire just like this one.

'My mother used to tell me about running past a shop window at the start of an air raid and the glass blowing out just behind her as a bomb dropped. We played in "bomb-sites" on the street where houses had stood; it was only later that I realized how terrifying every night must have been.'

ABOVE: Part of the pleasure of visiting living museums is the opportunity to travel on early forms of transport, such as the Gateshead no. 10 tramcar, built in 1925, and the replica Armstrong Whitworth car at Beamish. Public transport changed life fundamentally, allowing more people to travel for work or pleasure and to move further away from their birthplaces.

RIGHT: An ARP warden desperately listens for signs of life after a bomb has dropped in this setting from the Blitz Experience at the Imperial War Museum. The Experience powerfully recreates the horror of emerging from an air-raid shelter into a devastated landscape, where an ordinary street of minutes ago is reduced to piles of rubble.

products, groceries and greengrocery, sweets and tobacco, as well as haberdashery. The chemist's shop has the original fittings from a real shop, donated by the family who owned it when it closed in 1974; the shelves and bottles are still as they were when it was open, and the costumed shopkeeper still makes pills by tamping them into moulds. There is also an ironmonger's, full of the goods needed by the many industries of the area, a pawnbroker's, a 1930s fried fish shop and a baker's, recreated as in 1910, when customers could not only buy bread, but also a glass of British wine with biscuits for threepence.

At the Imperial War Museum, fixed and interactive exhibitions explore military and civilian life in the two World Wars. The Trench Experience recreates the dark, terrifying conditions of World War I trenches through a life-size model, complete with noises, smells and shocking glimpses of wounded men; an ominous ladder leads 'over the top' into No Man's Land. The Blitz Experience evokes the drama of a World War II bombing raid; reconstructions of a bombed street and air-raid shelter illustrate the dangers of war for non-combatants. The shelter's seats shake when a bomb lands nearby, and after the all-clear you emerge into a devastated, rubble-filled scene – an ARP warden urges you to hurry, and to beware of breathing dense smoke.

LIFE AND DEATH IN THE TRENCHES

Almost a century after its outbreak, we are still haunted by the horrors of World War I. The scale and nature of the slaughter, which affected virtually every family in Britain, are beyond modern comprehension, as is the innocent patriotism that drove so many young men to enlist in response to Kitchener's famous pointed finger. Almost an entire generation of young men were killed, from all walks of life. The older son of the 'upstairs' family of the *Edwardian House* television series could consider himself fortunate to avoid the likely fate in the trenches of his Edwardian counterparts. His real-life, 21st-century school and the Oxford college he was about to join – just one school and just one college – between them, in 1914–18, lost 700 young men in the conflict.

Modern re-enactment groups, such as the Great War Society, are more than likely to have among their members descendants of those who fought, and died, in the war itself – a poignant thought. They include people of all ages, from teenage boys to hardened senior officers, and use authentic equipment: Lee Enfield rifles, Vickers and Lewis machine guns, bayonets for fighting at close quarters and heavy, cumbersome respirators, to be put on in seconds in the event of a gas attack. Troops wear meticulously authentic uniforms, complete with tin helmets, puttees (gaiters made of wool, designed to support the lower leg), leather belts or webbing containing mess tins, water bottles and ammunition, and the correct insignia. Re-enactors often purchase authentic costumes and uniforms from militaria shops, to bring them even closer to those who fought and died. They train and carry out manoeuvres in their aim to get as close as possible to

*'Pack up your troubles in your old kit-bag,
 And smile, smile, smile.
While you've a lucifer to light your fag,
 Smile, boys, that's the style.
What's the use of worrying?
 It never was worth while, so
Pack up your troubles in your old kit-bag,
 And smile, smile, smile.'*

WORLD WAR I TROOP SONG

RIGHT: The Trench Experience at the Imperial War Museum assaults the senses with exploding flares and 'whizzbangs', heat and smells, all within the setting of a reconstructed trench. In this dugout an officer wrestles with a crackling field telephone, used to transmit orders and relay reports, while an exhausted colleague snatches some sleep.

what it was like to be a 'Tommy', and many make pilgrimages to the sites of the battles in France or Flanders.

Re-enactors establish camps and conduct manoeuvres at historically charged locations such as Richmond Castle in Yorkshire, used as a prison for the conscientious objectors – contemptuously called 'conchies' – who refused to fight. Their cell walls feature the poignant graffiti of prisoners who were facing the death sentence for their beliefs, although their sentences were later commuted to years of hard labour. It was

ABOVE: Men go 'over the top' as part of the Trench Experience at the Imperial War Museum. First-hand accounts of trench life recall the bodies, flooding, thick mud and rats. They convey the fear – and the hopeless resignation – of troops awaiting orders to scramble up the ladders and cross No Man's Land in the teeth of fire from machine guns and rifles, as well as shells.

then shameful to refuse to fight and to demonstrate for peace; white feathers of cowardice were offered to young civilian men not in uniform, while posters depicted young children asking 'What did you do in the war, Daddy?'

The horrors of conditions in the trenches, No Man's Land, gas shells and lethal 'advances' across small areas of ground have been powerfully chronicled in poems, writings and letters. Many of the great poets of World War I died during or soon after the conflict, among them Edward Thomas; Guillaume Apollinaire, who wrote that famous epitaph to the war: 'Ah Dieu! Que la guerre est jolie' ('Oh God! What a lovely war'); and Wilfred Owen, killed only a week before the Armistice in 1918. Owen's searing poems give powerful insight into the physical and psychological torment endured, sometimes for years on end, by officers and men on both sides of the conflict. The bleak humour of troops' songs provided a way of coping with the continual presence of death, as well as the extreme physical hardships. Huge rats were everywhere, the soldiers were infested with lice, and in hot weather swarms of flies gathered around the food and bodies. The debate still rages about a 'pardon' for soldiers, executed after being driven by the shelling, mustard gas and constant fear into a form of what we now recognize as post-traumatic stress disorder.

LEFT: Nurses staffing a casualty clearing station at a Kirby Hall re-enactment of the battle of Loos in 1915. Professionals and VADs worked in terrible conditions, dealing with men severely wounded by guns and shells as well as those suffering from poison gas. This weapon was used to dreadful effect by both sides at Loos, and the British Expeditionary Force sustained more than 61,000 casualties during the three weeks of the battle.

Loading and firing a Lewis gun

1 A special loading tool is used to position bullets correctly in the magazine of the Lewis gun, the first effective portable machine gun. It could hold up to 47 rounds.

2 The gun is set up in firing position. Its bipod at the front takes the weight of the heavy, air-cooled barrel, while the raised sights ensured accurate shooting.

3 Depressing the trigger produces automatic fire until the magazine empties – and magazines emptied quickly in an attack. Spare drums were held in special pouches or canvas buckets.

'My own beloved wife,
We are on the eve of a great action in
which I have been detailed to take a
dangerous part. … I am writing this
now in case I do not come out of it.
Dearest, you have been the best wife
a man could have had, and I was
very lucky to have won you. …
I hope if I go out I shall go decently
and do my duty manfully and well
before doing so.'

THE OFFICER WHO WROTE THIS LETTER WAS KILLED TWO
WEEKS LATER, AT THE BATTLE OF THE SOMME

Women were involved in the war as nurses in the medical field hospitals – a difficult and at times dangerous role, especially in casualty clearing stations close to the front line. Re-enactments today include stretcher parties who bring in the wounded to medical tents like those used in World War I, laying them on beds of the period and handing them over to doctors and nurses. The tents are stocked with blankets and the limited medical equipment of the time: surgical instruments, tourniquets, gauze and wool for bandages, splints for broken limbs, and peroxide, eusol and saline for disinfecting wounds.

The mindset of trench warfare is, fortunately, impossible to recapture, despite being less than a century old. A recent television programme took a group of volunteers back to life in the trenches, where they endured physical discomfort, poor food, heavy packs and mud. The contrast with 21st-century life and attitudes was striking, as was the men's anxiety when individuals failed to return from reconnaissance or wire-mending duties and had to be presumed dead. Nevertheless, without the daily encounters with death and injury, such re-enactment cannot approach the real experience or the almost tangible fear revealed in contemporary photographs and newsreels.

We have never entirely moved on from the suffering of the Great War. Even today, it is still almost impossible to visit the well-kept cemeteries of northern France or Flanders without dissolving into a mist of tears. Gone are the terrible sights of mud and blasted trees, flattened towns and villages, severed limbs, flooded shell holes and mud everywhere, but newly ploughed fields still regularly yield up a harvest of ironmongery: barbed wire, bullets, fragments of boots and gas masks, even unexploded shells, and one of those rather absurd German pointed helmets, pierced, impossibly sadly, by the bullet hole that would have certainly been fatal. Tours of the battlefields and cemeteries bring us closer to what happened then, to try to make sense of what seems inexplicable and still touches modern sensibilities.

.

WORLD WAR II – THE FIRST MODERN WAR

Only 20 years after the 'War to end all Wars', Europe was again engulfed in conflict. The advent of more modern weapons – more effective tanks, fighter planes, submarines and even Hitler's so-called 'wonder weapon' – the V2 rocket – made this perhaps the first recognizably modern war. So did the massive threat to civilians from aerial attacks and bombardments, and the shortages of food and goods caused by the targeting of supply-carrying ships. Traditional non-combatants became active participants, and women's contribution to the war effort was enforced by conscription into the forces, factories and on to the land. As a consequence, re-enactments of World War II, drawing as they do upon civilian as well as military life, offer varied roles to both men and women.

There are hundreds of World War II re-enactment societies in many countries, reflecting the global nature of the conflict. Most of them, as with World War I societies, recreate themselves as specific military units, wearing authentic uniforms and insignia, carrying the correct equipment and taking part in typical manoeuvres and actions (though battle re-enactments tend to be generic rather than attempts to recreate specific actions). Their kit is frequently genuine, and their devotion to detail meticulous. Appropriate military haircuts are specified and advice given on styles typical of the time and acceptable today; spectacles need to be rimless or wire-framed, and watches must be contemporary – no day/date features or digital displays. Modern World War II re-enactors are well groomed and tidy, and they never wear unearned military decorations.

There are dealers from whom tanks can be bought, and some re-enactment societies have them, though guns are obviously disabled. Original parachutes, which could not be steered and so drifted all over

'Many re-enactors of 20th-century warfare have real uniforms and equipment because they were manufactured in their millions ... the tanks are a bit pricey, though. One of the minor problems is haircuts ... you want to look right, but you don't want to look too out of place when you go back to work on Monday.'

BELOW: Re-enactment is an international activity. These American troops, members of the 2nd Armoured Division, are riding on board an M8 armoured car after a successful operation in Normandy during World War II. Dwindling numbers of serviceable vehicles from the war are kept going by enthusiasts, many of whom buy them and loan them to re-enactment groups.

the place, are too dangerous for use today, so a modern display team with square, steerable parachutes is hired if a re-enactment requires a parachute descent. Guns are also tightly regulated. Those used in modern re-enactments are of three types: blank-firing replicas, which make the right sound but do not fire real bullets; deactivated real weapons; or – in special circumstances and from a film armourer company – the real thing, quite capable of killing, with their use stringently controlled by the police.

As in World War I, women did join up as nurses, but they were also recruited into the services: the WRNS, the WAF and the ATS. Initially many were drivers, but later they took on other roles, such as members of anti-aircraft gun batteries. These roles are also re-enacted by today's societies, offering opportunities for all ages and both sexes to take part in operations from an evocative and recent part of history.

LIVING IN THE 1940S AND '50S

World War II invaded daily life. Women in their millions were recruited into war work in factories making munitions and essential goods, and by 1943 over 90,000 Land Girls, aged between 18 and 40, replaced male agricultural labour. Gardens were turned into allotments for vegetables as posters urged people to 'Dig for Victory', and rationing was introduced to combat food shortages – staples such as onions and tomatoes gradually disappeared after France and the Channel Islands fell to the Germans. Food was a major concern of the modern Hymers family – volunteers who returned to life in wartime Kent for a television programme, *The 1940s House*. They inhabited a real house of the period (17 Braemar Gardens, West Wickham, Kent, built in the early 1930s), under strict rules designed to ensure that nothing modern intruded. Local shops joined by recreating parts of their premises as shops of the time, offering only the goods that would have been available then – vegetables in their season, strictly rationed meat, replacements of the real thing such as dried egg.

The family wore period clothes at all times and they worked within a strict budget. An average wage for people living there at that time would have been around £350 a year, so the Hymers were only

ABOVE: A woman lays the table for family supper in the 1940s House, reconstructed at the Imperial War Museum. Food was either bought from local shops under strict rationing rules or grown in the garden. The windows behind her are taped against the danger of blast – a real risk in the actual Kent house, which lay under the flight path of German bombers heading for London.

LEFT: Getting in the harvest in the 1940s, recreated here at the Ryedale Folk Museum, was a very labour-intensive operation. A Grey Ferguson tractor draws an implement to cut the wheat, while behind a man clears away the crop with a pitchfork to prevent it being crushed in the tractor's next pass. More mechanized methods were starting to appear, but harvesting the hard way is well within living memory.

allowed to spend what would have been available to them out of that income. Everyday items were restricted: no more than 12.5 cm (5 inches) of water in baths, and low fires to conserve coal; the embers were sieved to save any reusable pieces. Although the Hymers each had a modern £20 note for real-life emergencies, hunger didn't count!

In the country these were the days before combine harvesters, when much of the labour on the land was manual. Horses were still employed to pull ploughs and scythes were used alongside tractors. Ryedale Folk Museum regularly recreates a 1940s harvest that requires about a dozen people to harvest just one field, with the help of horses to power the threshing machine. The day starts with four men cutting the corn with scythes, followed by teams of people who bind the crop into sheaves with corn ropes. The harvesters pile the sheaves into stooks to dry, prior to threshing by the horse wheel and winnowing to get rid of the chaff and weeds. Other re-enactors at Ryedale mill the corn and bake bread with the flour, all in one day.

Wartime austerity, including the rationing of food and clothes, continued well after the end of World War II, as Britain and much of Europe strove to rebuild their shattered economies. Despite the pace of change in later years, initially things took time. Old back-to-back houses were still inhabited, and many of the pit cottages recreated at places such as Beamish still relied on coal-fired ranges for cooking and hot water, and lacked flushing toilets. Lifestyles in the 1950s, when technological developments such as television, telephones and domestic appliances were just becoming available, seem far removed from all we take for granted today. Yet it was part of real life for millions of people. Anyone alive then can recall the days before supermarkets, when biscuits were bought by the pound from tins at the front of the grocery counter; when the vegetables available in the greengrocers did not include exotica such as red peppers or – heaven forbid – lemongrass; when a roast chicken was a Christmas treat.

Recent royal celebrations to mark the Queen's 50 years on the throne have created a new interest in the 1950s. Looking back at that period and the decades before only emphasizes how great the distance is – even such a short time ago – between then and now. At the same time it shows how important it is for us to seek to understand our history, both recent and more remote. This is the point of living history in all its forms – to make real attempts to touch the past and get close to the 'people like us' who lived then.

BELOW: The shelves of the village shop at Ryedale are restocked by the shopkeeper wearing the typical 'pinny' and turban of the time. Small local shops, vital to their communities when few people had cars, sold loose and packaged ingredients for meals cooked at home rather than prepared dishes. Brands such as Weetabix and Rowntrees Fruit Gums have survived, however, although the packaging has changed.

Useful Names and Addresses

The websites of English Heritage (www.english-heritage.org.uk) and of the National Archives in Kew (www.nationalarchives.gov.uk) are useful for information about some of Britain's most fascinating historic sites and documents.

Below (in alphabetical order) are contact details for some of Britain's best living museums, open air museums, living history groups and re-enactment societies.

LIVING MUSEUMS
By their nature, living museums and open air museums keep seasonal opening hours. Many hold special events, so check what is on and when if you are planning a visit.

Amberley Working Museum,
Houghton Bridge, West Sussex BN18 9LT
01798 831370;
email: office@amberleymuseum.co.uk;
website: www.amberleymuseum.co.uk

Beamish, The North of England Open Air Museum, Beamish,
County Durham DH9 0RG
0191 370 4000;
email: museum@beamish.org.uk;
website: www.beamish.org.uk

Bede's World, Church Bank,
Jarrow, Tyne and Wear NE32 3DY
0191 489 2106;
email: visitor.info@bedesworld.co.uk;
website: www.bedesworld.co.uk

Black Country Living Museum, Tipton Road, Dudley, West Midlands DY1 4SQ
0121 557 9643;
email: info@bclm.co.uk;
website: www.bclm.co.uk

Butser Ancient Farm, Nexus House, Gravel Hill, Waterlooville, Hants PO8 0QE
023 9259 8838; website: www.butser.org.uk

Chiltern Open Air Museum, Newland Park, Gorelands Lane, Near Chalfont St Giles, Buckinghamshire HP8 4AB
01494 871117;
email: coamuseum@netscape.net;
website: www.coam.org.uk

Dunaskin Open Air Museum,
Dalmellington Road, Waterside, Nr Patna, East Ayrshire, Scotland KA6 7JF
01292 531144;
email: dunaskin@btconnect.com;
website: www.dunaskin.org.uk

Flagship Portsmouth and Historic Dockyards, Porters Lodge, College Road, HM Naval Base, Portsmouth, Hampshire PO1 3LJ
01705 861512;
email: enquiries@flagship.org.uk;
website: www.flagship.org.uk

The Historic Dockyard,
Chatham, Kent ME4 4SX
01634 823800 or 01634 823807;
email: info@chdt.org.uk;
website: www.chdt.org.uk

Imperial War Museum,
Lambeth Road, London SE1 6HZ
020 7416 5000;
email: mail@iwm.org.uk;
website: www.iwm.org.uk

The Ironbridge Gorge Museum Trust,
Ironbridge, Telford, Shropshire TF8 7AW
01952 433522;
email: info@ironbridge.org.uk;
website: www.ironbridge.org.uk

JORVIK, Coppergate, York,
North Yorkshire, YO1 9WT
01904 543403;
email: enquiries@vikingjorvik.com;
website: www.vikingjorvik.com

Kentwell, Kentwell Hall,
Long Melford, Suffolk CO10 9BA
01787 310 207;
email: info@kentwell.co.uk;
website: www.kentwell.co.uk

The 1642 Living History Village of Little Woodham, Grange Farm, Howe Road, Rowner, Gosport, Hampshire
02392 377447 or 02392 520982;
email: roger@portsdown.fsnet.co.uk; website: www.portsdown.demon.co.uk/village.htm

Museum of East Anglian Life, Crowe Street, Stowmarket, Suffolk IP14 1DL
01449 612229;
email: pat@meal.fsnet.co.uk;
website: www.suffolkcc.gov.uk/tourism/meal

Museum of Welsh Life, St Fagans, Cardiff, South Glamorgan, Wales CF5 6XB
02920 573500; email: post@nmgw.ac.uk;
website: www.nmgw.ac.uk/mwl

Norfolk Rural Life Museum, Gressenhall, Dereham, Norfolk NR20 4DR
01362 860563 or 01362 869263;
email: gressenhall.museum@norfolk.gov.uk;
website:www.norfolk.gov.uk/tourism/museums/nrlm

The Peat Moors Centre, Shapwick Road, Westhay, near Glastonbury,
Somerset BA6 9TT
01458 860697; email:
ironage@peatmoors.freeserve.co.uk;website:w
www.somerset.gov.uk/levels/pmvc.htm

Ryedale Folk Museum, Hutton-le-Hole, York, North Yorkshire YO62 6UA
01751 417367;
email: info@ryedalefolkmuseum.co.uk;
website: www.ryedalefolkmuseum.co.uk

Warwick Castle, Warwick,
Warwickshire, CV34 4QU
(send enquiries to 'customer information')
0870 442 2000;
email: customer.information@warwick-castle.co.uk;
website: www.warwick-castle.com

Weald and Downland Open Air Museum, Singleton, Chichester, Sussex PO18 0EU
01243 811363;
email: office@wealddown.co.uk;
website: www.wealddown.co.uk

West Stow Country Park and Anglo-Saxon Village, Icklingham Road, West Stow, Bury St Edmunds, Suffolk IP28 6HG
01284 728718; email:
weststow@burybo.stedsbc.gov.uk;
website:
www.stedmundsbury.gov/weststow.htm

LIVING HISTORY SOCIETIES
There are literally hundreds of living history groups and re-enactment societies all over Britain. They range in size from a core of enthusiasts to internationally famous groups. The details below give a small selection to help you to find out where and when societies perform, and how you can become involved.

47th Regiment of Foot
Nigel Hardacre, 60 Oakcroft, Woodend, Clayton-le-Woods, Chorley, Lancs PR6 7UJ
01772 315192;
e-mail: nhardacre47@hotmail.com

Anmod Dracan
John Watson, Imladris, 224 Coatham Road, Redcar, Cleveland TS10 1RA
01642 489227;
e-mail: anmod.dracan@dtn.ntl.com

Arrowflight
Geoffrey Rhodes, 5 Mountain Row, Crane Moor Nook, Crane Moor, Sheffield,
West Yorkshire S35 7AN
0114 288 4707

Britannia
Dan Shadrake, 13 Ardleigh,
Basildon, Essex SS16 5RF
01268 544511;
e-mail: shadrake@blueyonder.co.uk;
website: www.durolitum.co.uk

Buckingham's Retinue
Chris Howell
e-mail: chris@the-retinue.freeserve.co.uk;
website: www.bucks-retinue.org.uk

Courteney Household & Co
Star House, Star Corner, Breage, Helston,
Cornwall TR13 9PJ
01326 562908

Diehard Company
Tim Rose, 21 Addison Way, North Bersted,
Bognor Regis, West Sussex PO22 9HY
01243 860036;
e-mail: tl.rose@virgin.net;
website: www.diehards.org.uk

Duelling Association
Baden Favill, 27 Mansell Drive, Aylestone,
Leicester, Leicestershire NE2 8PP
0116 233 7980;
e-mail: bwf@star.le.ac.uk

**ERA (formerly End of the
Roman Age Society)**
Matt Bunker, 14 Clive Road, Quinton,
Birmingham, West Midlands B32 1HN
0121 241 4917;
e-mail: mbtfx@aol.com;
website: www.erauk.org

Ermine Street Guard
Chris Haines, Oakland Farm, Dog Lane,
Crickley Hill, Whitcombe, Glos GL3 4UG
01452 862235;
e-mail: theESG@aol.com;
website: www.esg.ndirect.co.uk

Erpyngham Retinue
Chris Skinner, 28 Hindhead Point,
Wanborough Drive, Roehampton,
London SW15 4AW
020 8789 8483; e-mail/website:
chris@erpyngham-retinue.org.uk

Fairfax Battalia
Simon Frame, 81 Park Road,
Downend, Bristol, Avon BS16 5LQ
0117 5563392;
e-mail: www.fairfax.org.uk

Fauconberg Household
Mark Arnold, 6 Ridgeway, Aldridge, Walsall,
West Midlands WS9 0HL
01922 453166;
e-mail: roland@hyndfs.fsnet.co.uk

The Garrison
Jonathan Catton, c/o Tilbury Fort, Fort Road,
Tilbury, Essex RM18 7NR
01375 850484;
e-mail: jcatton@thurrock.gov.uk

The Great War Society
Brian Hicks, 13 Ashburton Road,
Westbury-on-Trym, Bristol, Avon BS10 5QN
0117 9042115;
website: www.thegreatwarsociety.co.uk

Hautbois
Rick and Helen Heavisides,
10A Greenholme Close, Langthorpe,
near Boroughbridge, Yorkshire YO51 9GA
01423 324369

Heuristics
Don Holton, PO Box 5514,
Matlock, Derbyshire DE4 5ZP
07860 966251;
e-mail/website: don@heuristics.org.uk

Historic Haute Cuisine
Annie Thompson, 105 Sandpit Lane,
St Albans, Hertfordshire AL4 0BW
01727 857444

History Re-enactment Workshop
Ruth Roberts, Hazel Cottage,
83 High Street, Billinghay, Lincs LN4 4ED
01526 861670;
website: www.historyreenactment.org.uk

Hogarth's Heroes
Stephen Wisdom
07976 765017;
email: ancient.abs@virgin.net

Lammas
Sarah Deere-Jones/Phil Williams, Trehawsa,
Whitstone, Holsworthy, Devon EX22 6TL
0776 2093443

Landsknechts
Linda Saxon, 1 Whitehouse Crescent,
Ashmore Park, Wednesfield, Wolverhampton,
West Midlands WV11 2HH
01902 682484;
e-mail: thepenfold@lineone.net

Livery & Maintenance
Phil Hill, 2 Pentillie Crescent, Mutley,
Plymouth, Devon PL4 6NY
01752 250780;
e-mail: phil@pjhill.plus.com

Medieval Siege Society
Chris Broome-Smith,
PO Box 105, Bexleyheath,
Kent DA7 4DL
020 8303 5640; e-mail/website:
www.medieval-siege-society.co.uk

Milites Litoris Saxonici
John Harris, 28 Elmsvale Road,
Dover, Kent CT17 9NT
01304 211492;
e-mail: jharris932@aol.com

Musica Antiqua
website: s-hamilton.k12.ia.us/antiqua

Napoleonic Association
Christine Binmore, 26 Copse Drive,
Wokingham, Berkshire RG41 1LX
0118 9783006;
e-mail: john.binmore@ntlworld.com;
website: www.n-a.co.uk

Past Pleasures
Mark Wallis, Abbots Cottage,
Portsmouth Road, St Catherine's,
Guildford, Surrey GU2 5EB
01483 450914;
e-mail: mark@pastpleasures.co.uk;
website: www.pastpleasures.co.uk

Plantagenet Medieval Society
Phil Pembridge, 27 Albemarle Road,
Churchdown, Gloucester,
Glos GL3 2HG
01452 713659;
e-mail: p.pembridge@aol.com

Quintains and Coronals
Stan Timbrell, 44 Middle Leasow,
Quinton, Birmingham, West Midlands
B32 1SW
0121 684 0545;
e-mail: quintains44@hotmail.com;
website: www.quintains.fsnet.co.uk

Raphael Falconry
Mike and Emma Raphael, 35 Chichester
Road, Halesworth, Suffolk IP19 8JL
01986 873928;
e-mail: raphaelfalconry@supanet.com;
website: www.raphaelfalconry.com

Regia Anglorum
Kim Siddorn, 9 Durleigh Close,
Headley Park, Bristol, Avon BS13 7NQ;
e-mail: kim.siddorn@blueyonder.co.uk;
website: www.regia.org

Ringwoods of History
Ralph Needham, 34 Sandford Road,
Mapperley, Nottingham, Notts NG3 6AL
0115 9692922

Roman Military Research Society
Jill Hatch, 24 Fouth Street,
Wilton, Salisbury, Wiltshire SP2 0JS
01722 556742;
e-mail: avrelia@hotmail.com;
website: www.romanarmy.net

Rosa Mundi
Claire Macdonald-Napier,
29 Holmefield View, Dane Hill Drive,
Holmewood, Bradford, W. Yorks BD4 0TJ
01274 661399;
website: www.rosamundi.org,uk

Sealed Knot
Anne Thomas,
Ty Ucha, Tan Y Fron, Abergele, Clwyd,
North Wales LL22 9AY; 01745 827033;
e-mail: info@sealedknot.org;
website: www.sealedknot.org

Siege Group
David Carvell, 1 Tyler Avenue,
Loughborough, Leics LE11 5NL
01509 558646;
e-mail: david.carvell@ntlworld.com;
website: www.siegegroup.co.uk

Silures Iron Age Society
Heather M Holt,
25 Anchorsholme Lane East,
Thornton-Cleveleys, Lancs FY5 3QH
Tel: 01253 852235;
e-mail: heather.holt@silures.fsnet.co.uk

Soutares and Clerces
Alex and Pam Summers,
107 Mongeham Road, Great Mongeham,
Deal, Kent CT14 0LJ
01304 381699;
e-mail: apsummers@eurobell.co.uk

Troop
Alan Larsen, 12 Chestnut House, Maitlands
Park Road, Chalk Farm, London NW3 2EE
e-mail: alanpeterlarsen@yahoo.co.uk

Viking Experience
website: www.viking-experience.co.uk

Vikings
Sandra Orchard, 2 Stanford Road,
Shefford, Bedfordshire SG17 5DS
01462 812208;
website: www.vikings.ndirect.co.uk

Wardour Garrison
Peter Hood, Hayes, Little Torrington,
Devon EX38 8PS
01805 622433;
email: hoodp@globalnet.co.uk

Winchester's Regiment of Foote
Nigel Cooper, 13 Chaffinch Drive,
Midsomer Norton, near Bath,
Somerset BA3 4NW
01761 418871;
e-mail: nigel.c.cooper@lineone.net;
website: www.marquisofwinchesters.co.uk

World War II Living History Association
David Bennett, 25 Olde Farm Drive,
Darby Green, Camberley, Surrey GU17 0DU
01252 409616;
e-mail: thames-solent@ntlworld.com;
website: www.ww2lha.com

Wynndebagge/The New St George Waits
Paul Saunders, 6 Swan Meadow,
Much Wenlock, Shropshire TF13 6JQ
01952 728283;
e-mail/website: info@wynndebagge.co.uk

York City Levy
Paul Morris, 54 Broadwell Road,
Easterside, Middlesbrough TS4 3NP
01642 273624

Further Reading

Alcock, **Joan**, *Life in Roman Britain*, B T Batsford/English Heritage, London, 1996

Best, **Nicholas**, *London: In the Footsteps of the Famous*, Bradt Travel Guides/English Heritage, Chalfont St Peter, 2002

Betjeman, **John**, 'Architecture' in Nowell-Smith, Simon (ed.), *Edwardian England: 1901–1914*, Oxford University Press, Oxford, 1964

Boardman, **A W**, *The Battle of Towton*, Sutton, Stroud, 1994

Brabbs, **Derry**, *England's Heritage*, Cassell & Co/English Heritage, London, 2001

Bradbury, **Jim**, *The Medieval Archer*, The Boydell Press, Woodbridge, 2002

Carlton, **Charles**, *Going to the Wars: the Experience of the English Civil Wars, 1638–1651*, Routledge, London, 1992

Cattell, **John & Hawkins**, **Bob**, *The Birmingham Jewellery Quarter: an Introduction and Guide*, English Heritage, London, 2000

Colwell, **Stella**, *The National Archives: An Introduction for Family Historians*, National Archives, London, 2003

Cox, **Jane**, *New to Kew?*, Public Record Office, London, 1999

Cox, **Margaret**, *Life and Death in Spitalfields 1700–1850*, Council for British Archaeology, York, 1996

Cunliffe, **Barry**, *Roman Bath*, B T Batsford/English Heritage, London, 1984

Davies, **Norman**, *The Isles*, Macmillan, London, 1999

Davis, **Norman (ed)**, *The Paston Letters* (pbk), Oxford University Press, Oxford, 1983

Davison, **Brian**, *Picturing the Past through the Eyes of Reconstruction Artists*, English Heritage/Cadw, London, 1997

Gardiner, **Juliet**, *The 1940s House*, Channel 4 Books, London, 2000

Gardiner, **Juliet**, *The Edwardian Country House*, Channel 4 Books, London, 2002

Giles, **John**, *The Somme Then and Now*, Battle of Britain Prints International, London, 1986

Guest, **Ken & Denise**, *British Battles*, HarperCollins/English Heritage, London,1996

Hallam, **Elizabeth**, *Domesday Souvenir Guide*, Public Record Office, London, 2000

Hardy, **Robert**, *Longbow. A Social and Military History*, Patrick Stephens, Yeovil, 2000

Hey, **David**, *How our Ancestors Lived*, Public Record Office, London, 2002

Hills, **Catherine**, *Blood of the British*, George Philip/Channel 4, London, 1986

Horsler, **Val**, *Royal Heritage*, English Heritage, London, 2002

Hussey, **Maurice**, *Chaucer's World: a Pictorial Companion*, Cambridge University Press, Cambridge, 1967

Lacey, **Robert & Danziger**, **Danny**, *The Year 1000*, Little Brown, London, 1999

McAleavy, **Tony**, *Life in a Medieval Abbey*, English Heritage, London, 1996

McAleavy, **Tony**, *Life in a Medieval Castle*, English Heritage, London, 1998

McAleavy, **Tony**, *Life in Roman Britain*, English Heritage, London, 1999

O'Shea, **Stephen**, *Back to the Front*, Robson Books, London, 1997

Peterson, **Daniel**, *The Roman Legions Recreated in Colour Photographs*, Crowood Press, Marlborough, 1992

Picard, **Liza**, *Restoration London*, Phoenix Press, London, 2001

Picard, **Liza**, *Dr Johnson's London*, Phoenix Press, London, 2001

Richards, **Julian**, *Blood of the Vikings*, Hodder & Stoughton, London, 2001

Ryley, **Claire**, *Roman Gardens and their Plants*, Fishbourne Roman Palace, Chichester, 1994

Schama, **Simon**, *A History of Britain. At the Edge of the World? 3000BC – AD1603*, BBC Worldwide Limited, London, 2000

Schama, **Simon**, *A History of Britain. The British Wars, 1603–1776*, BBC Worldwide Limited, London, 2001

Severs, **Dennis**, *18 Folgate Street: The Tale of a House in Spitalfields*, Chatto & Windus, London, 2001

Simpson, **Andy**, *Hot Blood and Cold Steel*, Tom Donovan, London,1993

Spurling, **Hilary**, *Elinor Fettiplace's Receipt Book: Elizabeth Country House Cooking*, Viking Salamander, London, 1986

Welch, **Martin**, *Anglo-Saxon England*, B T Batsford/English Heritage, London, 1992

Wood, **Eric S**, *Historical Britain*, Harvill, London, 1995

Plus the guidebooks and websites for English Heritage, National Trust and privately-run properties open to the public, as well as those of the living museums and open air museums.

Index Numbers in *italics* refer to illustrations and captions

A

Adam, Robert *20*, 110, 134, *134*, *135*
Aella 65, 78, *78*
Amberley Working Museum 24, 154
American troops, WW2 *182*, *183*
Anderida *see* Pevensey Castle
Anglo-Saxon Chronicle 68, 78
Anglo-Saxons *see* Saxons
animals
    industrial use *163*
    see also horses; livestock
Appuldurcombe House *133*
Aquae Sulis (Bath) 42, *46*, 47-8
archaeology, experimental 49
    see also farming
armour
    Roman *38*, *39*, *40*, *43*, *45*, 52, *53*, 54, *54*, *55*
    Romano-British 65
    Anglo-Saxon *79*, 81-2, *81*
    Viking 69
    medieval *87*, 99-100, *100*
    see also clothes and fashion; helmets; uniforms
Art Deco *174*
Audley End House 110, *110*, *111*, 117, *118*, 134
Aydon Castle 90

B

Bath
    Aquae Sulis 42, *46*, 47-8
    Georgian 134, *134*, *135*
baths, Roman 42, *44*, *46*, 47-9
Battle Abbey *82*
battle tactics
    hand-to-hand combat 57
    testudo *28*, 52, 54
battles
    Roman *28*, 52, 54, 56
    Viking and Saxon *28*, *77*, 78, *78*, *80*, *83*
    medieval *76*, 91, 101, *101*
    Civil War *123*, *124*, *125*
    Georgian period *144*, 145-6
    Victorian age *159*
    WW1 *180*
    WW2 *183*
    Culloden 145-6
    Edgehill 112
    Flodden 123
    Hastings 64, 70, *80*, 81, 82-3, *83*
    Larissa *76*, *101*
    Loos *180*
    Marston Moor 112
    Naseby 112
    Towton 91
    Waterloo, sketch map *147*
    see also weapons
Bayeux Tapestry 8, *77*, 81
Bazalgette, Sir Joseph 154
Beamish, The North of England
Open Air Museum 24, 36, *138*, 164-5, *166*, 176, *177*, 185
    blacksmith 165
    Clydesdale heavy horses *167*
    pit pony *163*
    Steam Elephant *148*, *152*, 164
Bede 68, *72*
Bede's World, Jarrow *23*, 24, 36, *67*, 68, 73-5, *73*
Beeston Castle 108
Berwick-upon-Tweed 131
Bess of Hardwick 110
Bignor 42
Birmingham
    canal system 137
    Jewellery Quarter 155, *155*
Black Country Living Museum,
Dudley 24, 36, *136*, 137, *162*, 163-4, *172*, 176-7, *176*
Black Death 87, 103
blacksmiths 165, 166
Blenheim Palace 33, 134
Blists Hill 23-4, *23*, *137*, *160*, 161-2, *161*, *164*
Bodiam Castle 90
Bodleian Library, Oxford 31
Bolsover Castle 110, *110*, 116-17, *116*, 144
border castles 90
Bowood House 134
bows
    arrow-tips *96*
    bow makers *29*
    crossbows 102, *102*
    longbows *29*, 90, *91*, 101-2
Box Hill Tunnel 153
    bill *153*
British Library 31
Brodsworth Hall *20*, *21*, *150*, 156, *156*
Brown, 'Capability' 110, 133-4, *133*, *134*
Brunel, Isambard Kingdom 152-3, *153*
Burgh Castle 66
Butser Ancient Farm, Hampshire 24-5, 36, *48*, 49, *49*
    Roman villa 50
Byland Abbey 92

C

Cadw (Wales) 32
Caerleon 42
Call to Arms 35
canal system 137, *162*, 163-4, *163*
cannons *107*, 109
Canterbury
    Cathedral 93
    St Martin's church 66
Carisbrooke Castle *98*, *99*, *108*, 109
Carlisle Castle 98, 130-1
Castle Acre Priory *81*, *192*
Castle Drogo 174
castles *178*, 179, *192*
    medieval 89-90
cathedrals
    medieval 93
    Norman *71*, *72*, *72*
cavalry *see* horsemanship
Cavendish family 110, *110*, 116-17
Charles I *108*, 109, 116-17, *116*
    estate inventory 1650 *37*
Charles II 117, *117*
Chatham Historic Dockyard 37, 109, *109*, 132, 159
    ropery *132*
    Wooden Walls 37, 132, *132*
Chaucer, Geoffrey, *The Canterbury Tales* 87
Chedworth 42
Chester, Rows 88
children *14*, *146*, *147*, *169*, *172*
Chiltern Open Air Museum 138, 165-6
Chippendale, Thomas *20*
Chiswick House *129*, 134
The church, medieval 92-4
churches, Saxon 66
Chysauster, Cornwall *21*, 50
Civic Trust 33
Civil War 106-25
    re-enactments 112, 122-4, *123*, *124*
Clare, Richard and Katharine *119*, 120, *120*
Cleeve Abbey 92, *93*
clothes and fashion
    Iron Age *11*, *22*, *51*
    Roman *47*, 57-9
    Anglo-Saxon *73*
    Georgian *135*, 139, *139*, *140*, *141*, *142*
    medieval *85*, *98*, *99*, *100*
    Tudor *112*, *113*, *114*
    Stuart 116, 117, *120*
    Victorian *168*, *169*
    see also armour; hairstyles; headgear; uniforms
Clydesdale heavy horses *167*
Coalbrookdale *see* Ironbridge
Colchester, Roman shop 59-60
cooking *see* food; kitchens
Corbridge, Roman re-enactments 35, *43*, 52
Corpus Christi College,
Cambridge, Parker Library 31
cosmetics, Roman 57-8
country houses, Georgian 133-5
country living
    Romans in Britain 49-51
    medieval 94
    Georgian times 138-9
    Victorian age 165-9
Courtauld, Stephen and Virginia *174*, 175
crafts
    Roman *61*
    Iron Age *11*, 50, *51*
    Anglo-Saxon *74*
Norman 74
Middle Ages *29*, *94*, *98*
Tudors *122*
Victorian *161*, *165*, 166
Cragside 156
cricket 142-3, *142*, *143*
Crossness pumping station 154, *154*
Culloden, battle of 145-6
curing skins *11*
curse tablets *46*, *47*
Cuthbert, Saint *72*

D

Darby, Abraham *136*
Darwin, Charles 156, *157*
Deal 134-5
Deal Castle 108, *113*
Diehards (Middlesex Regiment) *159*
dockyards *see* Chatham; Portsmouth
documents 30-1
    interpretation 37
documents from National Archives
    battle of Waterloo sketch *147*
    Box Hill Tunnel bill *153*
    Charles I estate inventory 1650 *37*
    cholera outbreaks *154*
    confession of Guy Fawkes *30*
    curse tablets *46*, *47*
    Dick Turpin's indictment *129*
    Great Plague, record of riot *18*
    John Bull poster *178*
    letter from soldier, WW1 *31*
    parchment scroll, Roman *61*
    Press Gang *131*
    signatures of Gunpowder Plot conspirators *30*
    Vindolanda shopping list tablet *44*
    see also Domesday Book
Domesday Book 64, 65, 71-2, *71*, *94*
Dover, Roman lighthouse 43
Dover Castle *32*, 112-13, *112*, 175, *175*
Down House 156, *157*
'Drengham' *79*
dress *see* clothes and fashion
Dudley family *113*, 114-15, *115*
Dunaskin Open Air Museum 162
Durham Cathedral *72*, *72*, 93

E

Edgehill, battle of 112
Edward I 96-7
Edward II *92*
Edward IV 91
The Edwardian Country House 173-4
Elizabeth I 106, 113-14, *114*
Eltham Palace *174*, 175, *192*
English Heritage 32, 33
Ermine Street Guard *28*, *38*, *39*, *40*,

42, 52
Etal Castle 107
Exeter Cathedral 93
experimental archaeology, Butser 49

F
farmhouses *19*, *94*, 96
farming *138*
    experimental 49, 73-4
    harvest *17*, *119*, *184*, 185
    see also livestock
fashion *see* clothes and fashion
Fawkes, Guy, confession *30*
First World War *31*, *33*, *170*, 172,
    178-82, *178*, *179*, *180*, *181*
    see also Great War Society
Fishbourne 42, 51, 52, 61
Flodden, battle of 123
food and drink
    Anglo-Saxons *67*, 74, *192*
    Georgian *137*, *138*, 147
    Iron Age *49*
    medieval period 103, *103*
    Norman Britain 75-6
    preparation *95*, *103*, *121*, *168*
    Roman Britain *47*, 59-61, *59*, *60*
    Stuart picnic *2*, *105*
    Stuarts *105*
    tea-making *118*
    Tudors and Stuarts *109*, 118-19,
    192
    Victorian *166*
    1940s *184*, *184*
    1950s *185*
    see also kitchens
footwear
    medieval *103*
    Roman sandals *58*
forges *162*
Fort Brockhurst *159*
47th Regiment of Foot (living
    history society) *13*
Fountains Abbey 92
Framlingham Castle 89

G
gardens, Victorian *166*
George II *127*, *192*
Georgian period 126-47
    re-enactments 136-8
Gladstone, William 150
Glasgow 174
Glastonbury 93-4
    'Lake Village' 49, 50, *50*
Gloucester Abbey 92
Gosport, Living Village of Little
    Woodham 36, 121-2, *122*
Gosport Advanced Line 159
Gosport Living History Society 121
Great Plague, record of riot *18*
Great War Society *33*, *170*, 178,
    178
    see also First World War
Gressenhall, Museum of Rural Life,
    Norfolk *24*, 138, 167, *168*, *169*
Gunpowder Plot, conspirators'
    signatures *30*
Gwynne, Nell 117, *117*

H
Haddon Hall 20, 21
Hadrian 58
Hadrian's Wall 42, *42*, 43-5, *44*, *45*,
    52
hairstyles
    Georgian 139
    Roman 57, 58
    Stuart 117, *117*
    see also clothes and fashion
Hampton Court 34, 110
Harewood House *20*
Hastings, battle of 64, 70, *80*, 81,
    82-3, *83*
headgear
    hats *3*
    medieval *85*
    Roman *53*
    see also hats; helmets
health
    cholera outbreak *154*
    Roman period 48
hearths 49-50, *49*, *62*
helmets *39*, *43*, *45*, *53*, *54*, *63*, *69*,
    81, 100-1, *100*, *124*, *125*, *159*, *178*
    see also armour; headgear
Helmsley Castle 108
Henrietta Maria, Queen 116-17,
    116
Henry VIII *107*, 108, 110, 112,
    112-13, *113*
Hereford Cathedral, Chained
    Library 31
Heritage Open Days 33
Herstmonceux Castle 103
Heuristics Group *93*
Historic Royal Palaces 33
Historic Scotland 32
History Re-enactment Workshop
    120
horsemanship
    jousting 98
    Norman *70*, *83*
    Roman 54
horses
    horse and cart as transport *23*
    horse dressing *167*
    pit ponies *163*
    as status symbols *73*
    working horses *17*, *23*, *138*, *167*
Housesteads 43, 44, *44-5*, 57
Hurst Castle 159

I
Imperial War Museum 24, 177-8
    1940s house *36*, 184, *184*
    Blitz Experience 177, *177*, *192*
    Trench Experience 177, *179*,
    180
industrial life
    Georgian 136-8, *137*
    Victorian *148*, *150*, 152-5, *154*,
    155
industrial museums 36
interpreters *see* re-enactment and re-
    enactors
Iron Age *11*, *22*, 25, *50*, *51*
    settlements *21*, 49-50

Ironbridge 136-7, *136*
    see also Blists Hill

J
James Watt & Co 154
Jekyll, Gertrude 174
jewellery 47, 67-8, *85*, 115, *115*
Jorvik Viking Centre, York 23, 37,
    70, 76-7, *77*
Jorvik Viking Festival *26*, *76*, 77-8,
    77, 80
'Juncina, Sosia' 61

K
Kedleston Hall 134
Keighley and Worth Valley Railway
    153
Kenilworth Castle *16*, *113*, 114-15
Kent, William 133, 134
Kentwell Hall 112, *125*
Kenwood House 134
Kirby Hall 116, *192*
    Civil War re-enactment *124*, *125*
    Landsknechts *108*
    Peninsular War re-enactment *19*,
    146-7, *146*, *147*
    Roman chariot races 57
    Roman re-enactment *28*, *38*, *39*,
    40
    Stuart picnic *2*, *105*
    WWI re-enactment *31*, *180*,
    181
    WWII re-enactment *171*
kitchens 20, 36, *150*, 176
    cooking hearths 49-50, *49*, *62*
    see also food

L
Landsknechts *108*
language, re-enactments and 121
Larissa, battle of *76*, *101*
Laxton, Nottinghamshire 94
Legio XIIII Gemina Martia Victrix
    40, 54
Legio XX Valeria Victrix *28*, *38*, *39*,
    40, *43*, *192*
Leighton House 156
letter writing, WWI *31*
Lewis gun *33*
Lincoln 86, 88-9
    Cathedral *86*, 93
    Roman gate *41*
Lindisfarne 64, 68-9
    Castle 174
    Priory 67
Little Woodham *see* Gosport
livestock, traditional and rare breeds
    10, 36, 49, *67*, 74, *75*, *103*, *138*,
    166, 167, *169*
living history events 33-5
living museums 23-5, 35-7, 176-7
London, Georgian 135
Longleat 33
Loos, battle of *180*
lorica segmentata *43*, 54, *55*
Lullingstone Roman villa 42
Lutyens, Sir Edwin 174
Lyddington Bede House *13*, *131*

M
Mackintosh, Charles Rennie 174
MacLeod, Clan 69
mail *81*
    see also armour
Manderston 173-4
manuscripts *see* documents
Manx National Heritage 32
Marble Hill House *3*, *15*, *126*, *134*,
    140, *141*, *192*
marriage, Norman *64*
Marston Moor, battle of 112
Martello towers 131-2
Mary Rose 109, *109*
medieval life 84-103
Medieval Siege Society 34, 102, *103*
mercenaries, Landsknechts *108*
mines *162*
monks *93*
Morgan, Len 26, 34, 54
mosaics, Roman *41*
Mount Grace Priory 92-3
Mucking (village) 64
Museum of East Anglian Life,
    Stowmarket, Suffolk 24, 36, 139,
    166
Museum of Welsh Life, Cardiff 24,
    94, 96, 137, 139
    Hendre'r-ywydd Uchaf
    farmhouse *94*, 96
museums, living history 35-7
music and musical instruments *12*,
    15, *16*, *34*, *56*, 98, *112*, 141-2,
    141, *171*, *192*
Musica Antiqua 98

N
Naseby, battle of 112
National Archives (previously
    Public Record Office) 30, 37
    see also documents from National
    Archives
National Army Museum *31*
National Trust 32-3
National Trust for Scotland 32-3
Neolithic trackway *22*
New Forest *70*
New Lanark 137
New Model Army *124*, *125*
Newcomen engine house *136*, 137,
    163
The 1900 House 160
1920s *176*
1930s *174*, 175, *192*
1940s house *see* Imperial War
    Museum
1950s 185
Norfolk Rural Life Museum,
    Gressenhall 24, 36
Norham Castle 107
Normans 62-83
    re-enactments 37, 70, *70*, *76*, 81,
    101, *192*
North of England Open Air
    Museum *see* Beamish, the North
    of England Open Air Museum
nursing wounded soldiers *19*, *146*,
    180, *181*

O

occupations *see* crafts
Offa's Dyke Path 68
Old Sarum *71*
Orboch, Isle of Skye 69
Orderic Vitalis 71
Orford 89-90
Osborne House 158, *158*
Osterley Park 134
Our Lady of Walsingham 93
Owen, Wilfred 180

P

Paddington Station 153
Papplewick water pumping station 154
parchment scroll, Roman *61*
Parker, Matthew 31
Paston letters 87
Peat Moors Centre, Somerset 11, *22*, 25, *25*, 36, 49-50, *50*, *51*
Pendennis Castle *107*, 108, 175
Peninsular Wars re-enactment *19*, 146-7, *146*, *147*, *159*
Pepys, Samuel 119
Percy family *89*
Pevensey Castle (Anderida) 43, 52, *65*, 66, *66*, *78*
pilgrimage sites 93-4
Pimperne, Iron Age house 50
pit ponies *163*
Pockerley Manor 164
population changes 17
Portchester Castle 66, 142-3, *142*, *143*
Portsmouth 133, 159
    Historic Dockyard 37, 109, *130*, 132-3
poultry *67*, 103, *138*, *166*
Press Gang document *131*
Public Record Office *see* National Archives
pugio *43*
Pulteney Bridge, Bath *134*, *135*
pumping stations 154

R

railways 153-4
rare breeds *see* farming
Ravenglass and Eskdale Railway 153
re-enactment and re-enactors 26-9, *27*, *97*
    fairs 34-5
    societies 34
    Romans in Britain 52-61
    Saxons, Normans and Vikings 73-83
    medieval 95-103
    Tudors and Stuarts 112-25
    Georgian 136-47
    Victorian 160-9
    20th-century 176-85
Reculver 66
Regia Anglorum *5*, 37, 79-80
Ribblehead Viaduct 153
Richborough *40*, *41*, 42-3, 52, *56*, *57*, *59*, 60, 66, *78*

Richmond Castle 70
    WWI re-enactment *33*, *170*, *178*, 179
Rievaulx Abbey 92
roads, Neolithic trackway 22
Romans in Britain 38-61
    country living 49-51
    town living 47-8
Roman army 26, *28*, *35*, *38*, *39*, 42-7, *47*, 52-77
    cornucen 56
    optio 54
    signum 52, *55*
    tent *58*
Roman baths 42
Roman Britain 38-61
Roman Military Research Society *40*, 54, 61
Roman mosaics *41*
Roman villas 50-1
Romano-British crafts 50
Romano-British fighters *65*, *78*
roundhouses 48, 49-50, *50*, *51*
royal progresses
    medieval 96
    Stuart 116-17
    Tudor 112-14, *113*, *114*
rural life, Georgian period 138-9
Ryedale Folk Museum 24, *95*, 103, 139, 166, *166*, *185*
    1940s harvest *17*, *184*, 185
    pigs *10*
Ryngley, Sir Edward *113*

S

St Mawes Castle *107*, 108
St Pancras Station 153
Saltash, Royal Albert Bridge 152-3
Saxons 62-83
    re-enactors *56*, *57*, *67*
Saxon Shore forts 42, *56*, 66
Second World War *171*, 172, 175, *175*, 182-4
    Kirby Hall re-enactment *182*, *183*
Settle-Carlisle line 153
sewers 154
ships
    Gannet 159
    Mary Rose 109
    Valiant 132
    Victory 130, 132-3
    Warrior 159
    see also Viking longships
shops *24*, 59-60, *160*, 166, 177, *184*, 185
Silchester 47
Sir John Astley's Regimente of Foote 28
Skara Brae, Orkney 22
Smithson, John (architect) *110*
smocking *169*
Smythson, Robert (architect) *110*
Somerset House 130
Somerset Levels *see* Peat Moors Centre, Somerset
Spitalfields Trust 135
Spitfires (1940s tribute band) *171*
sport

Georgian, cricket 142-3
jousting *82*, *89*, 98-9, *98*, *99*, *192*
Roman chariot racing *57*
Viking rowing races *76*, *77*
Spurling, Hilary 118
Stamford 134
Stephenson, George 164
Stokesay Castle *88*, 90-1
Stowe 134
Stuarts 106-25
    re-enactments 116-17
Suffolk, Countess of *118*, *140*
Sutton Hoo 67-8, *68*

T

Tacitus 55, 59
tent, Roman *58*
Tewkesbury Battlefield Society 102
thatching *122*
tinsmiths *164*
Tower of London 34
    White Tower 70
Towton, battle of 91
Towton Battlefield Society 91, 102
transport
    horse and cart *23*
    Neolithic trackway 22
    tractors *184*
    tramcar *177*
    see also canal system
Trevithick, Richard *137*
Tudors 106-25
    re-enactments 112, 113-15
Tunbridge Wells *128*, *135*, *137*
    Georgian Week 34
    Pantiles *12*
Turpin, Dick, indictment *129*
Twentieth century (early) 170-85
Tynemouth Priory *192*
Tyntesfield 156

U

uniforms
    Civil War *125*
    Georgian *13*, 144
    Victorian *159*
    WWI 178, *178*
    see also armour
Upnor Castle *109*
urban life
    Georgian 134-5
    Roman 47-8
    Victorian 160-5

V

Victoria, Queen *149*, 150
Victorian period 148-69
Viking longships *76*
    figurehead *26*
    ship-burning *5*, *78*
Vikings 62-83
    longships *5*, *26*, *76*, *78*
    re-enactors and re-enactments 37, *63*, *69*, *76*, *77*, *192*
Vindolanda 44, *44*

W

Waist, Joan of Derby 106
Wales, heritage railways 153
Walker, Samuel and Hannah *104*, *119*, *121*
Walmer Castle 113, *113*
Warkworth Castle, Northumberland *89*
Wars of the Roses 100-1
    Yorkist soldiers *84*, *87*, 91
warships *see* ships
Warwick Castle 23, 33, 34, *90*
Waterloo, battle of, sketch *147*
wattling and daubing *25*, 48, 50, *51*, *94*
Weald and Downland Museum 96, 119-21, 138, 139, 165-6, 169
    Bayleaf Farmstead 96
    Pendean Cottage and Farm *14*, *36*, *119*, *120*
    Poplar Cottage *104*, *106*, 169
weapons
    Roman *43*, *56*, *57*
    Norman *80*, *81*, *83*
    Saxon *77*, *78*, *80*, 81, *83*
    Viking *77*, *78*
    medieval *29*, *90*, *91*, *96*, 101-2, *102*
    Tudor and Stuart *107*, *109*
    Civil War developments 122-4, *123*
    Georgian 144-5, *144*, *145*
    Victorian *159*
    WWI *33*, *178*, *178*, *181*
    WWII 182-3, *182*
    see also battles
weaving 50, *51*, *74*, *75*
Wenlock Priory 93
West Stow Anglo-Saxon village 24, 36, 37, *62*, 64, 66-7, 74-6, *192*
Wharram Percy *94*
Wheeldale Moor 41
'Wichamstow' 79
William I 64, 66, 70-1
Winchester Cathedral *17*
Witley Court *173*
women, in re-enactments *19*, *36*, *47*, *64*, *77*, *85*, *90*, *180*, 181, 183, 184
Woodchester *41*
Wooden Walls *see* Chatham historic dockyard
World Wars *see* First World War; Second World War; *also* World War I, World War II
Wren, Sir Christopher 110
Wrest Park *106*, *133*
Wroxeter *41*, 47
'Wychurst' 37, 80-1

Y

Yeavering 68
York
    Castle 70-1
    Shambles 88
    see also Jorvik
Yorkshire, monasteries 92

Acknowledgements

This book is as much Derry Brabbs' as mine; it is a privilege for me to have my words associated with his photographs, and I am immensely grateful for his help with the detail of the images as well as for the superb photographs themselves. And then there is Catherine Bradley, editor *extraordinaire*, whose vision and care made the book what it is and to whom I owe a huge debt of gratitude; David Starkey who has honoured the book with a Foreword; and Nigel Soper whose elegant design has helped to capture the spirit of living history.

There are so many people whose help has been invaluable: at the publishers, Michael Dover for his initial and continued belief in the book and in me, and at English Heritage, huge support from Tracy Borman, Kellie Blake and Mark Selwood. I am grateful to Professor Barry Cunliffe at the Institute of Archaeology, Oxford, and, for researching illustrations, to Celia Sterne at the English Heritage picture library, Alyson Rogers at the National Monuments Record and Wendy Adamson at the British Museum. Particular thanks are also due to Jane Crompton, Paul Johnson and Hugh Alexander at the National Archives in Kew (formerly the Public Record Office) for their enthusiasm and assistance in sourcing documents.

The re-enactors and costumed interpreters to whom I spoke were unfailingly generous in imparting their well-researched wisdom: Andy Dornan, medieval historian and crossbowman *nonpareil*; Len Morgan, impressive Roman centurion and armourer; Alan Larsen, jouster and all-round, multi-period warrior and horseman; Kim Siddorn who happily imparted his devotion to the Viking Age; Julian Humphreys, omniscient soldier; Mark Wallis of Past Pleasures and his team of costumed actors (who have featured in many of the photographs in the book), especially Rosanna Summers and Mike Bradley; Tina Fowler, Civil War pikewoman; Chris and Stacey Skinner for medieval knights, Paul Saunders for insights into medieval music and Don Holton for other medieval lore; David Bennett and Geoff Carefoot for 20th-century militaria ... These are just some of those who were generous with their help and expert knowledge.

I would also like to thank the many staff and volunteers in museums of living history and open air museums who have contributed their time, enthusiasm and expertise so generously. There are too many to thank everyone individually, but their knowledge and help has been most appreciated. Special thanks are due to Jenny Barnes at the Ryedale Folk Museum; Elizabeth Bowers at the Imperial War Museum; Trish Hall at Beamish; Helen Mitchell at the Norfolk Rural Life Museum, Gressenhall; Emma Middleton and Amanda Nash at the Black Country Living Museum; Gillian Neild at Heritage Projects on behalf of JORVIK; Meinwen Ruddoch at the Museum of Welsh Life; Christine Shaw and colleagues at Butser Ancient Farm; Laura Sole at Bede's World and, last but by no means least, Eddie Wills at the Peat Moors Centre.

The publishers would also like to thank Slaney Begley, Drusilla Calvert, Kathleen Gill, Justin Hunt and Austin Taylor for their help in the preparation of this book. They would also like to acknowledge the help of Spectrum, who represents the actors featured in the photographs on pages 36 (bottom), 177 (bottom) and 184 (top).

Text acknowledgements
The quotation by John Betjeman on page 173 is from 'Architecture', his contribution to Simon Nowell-Smith (ed.), *Edwardian England: 1901–1914*, page 362, Oxford University Press, 1964. The quotation from the Paston letters on page 31 is from the World's Classics edition, edited by Norman Davies and published by Oxford University Press in 1983. Both are reproduced by permission of Oxford University Press.

The quotations on pages 146–7 are from the joint letter written by Edward and William Freer to their father during the Peninsular Wars. The letter appears in *Letters from the Peninsula: The Freer Family Correspondence 1807–1814*, by Norman Scarfe MA, published by University College Leicester in 1953, and subsequently republished on the Internet by kind permission of the Leicester Archaeological Society. The words of Edward appear in the main text on pages 146–7, those of his brother in the caption on page 146; their joint letter is dated 14 April 1812.

Photographic acknowledgements
The publishers would like to thank the people, living museums and organizations listed below for permission to reproduce the photographs in this book. Every care has been taken to trace copyright holders, but any omissions will, if notified, be corrected in any future edition.

All photographs are © Derry Brabbs with the exception of the following:

Beamish, The North of England Open Air Museum: 138; Black Country Living Museum: 136 bottom right; British Museum: 44 bottom right; Butser Ancient Farm 48–9; Chatham Historic Dockyard: 132 bottom; Jarrolds Publishing and Chatham Historic Dockyard: 132 top; Trustees of the Imperial War Museum: 178 bottom left; 179; 180 top; Institute of Archaeology, Oxford: 46 right; Museum of Welsh Life: 19 top; 94 bottom; 154 bottom; Portsmouth Historic Dockyard: 109 top; 130; Ryedale Folk Museum (Jenny Barnes): 10; 17 bottom; 95; 166 bottom; VIPS–Paul Eddom: 5.

Reproduced by permission of English Heritage picture library: 17 top (John Critchley); 21 c Skyscan balloon photography; 32 (Jeremy Richards); 41 left (Paul Highnam), right (Jonathan Bailey); 44 bottom left: (Jeremy Richards); 45 top (c Skyscan balloon photography; 60 top right (Bob Skingle); 66 c Skyscan balloon photography; 86 (John Critchley); 88 (John Wyand); 89 top (Nigel Corrie); 107 bottom (Nigel Corrie); 108 bottom (Jonathan Bailey); 109 bottom; 110 top (Pat Payne); 111 (Paul Highnam); 113 bottom (Andrew Tryner); 116 bottom (Jonathan Bailey); 133 top (Paul Highnam), bottom (John Critchley); 150 (Paul Highnam); 156 (John Critchley); 157 (Jonathan Bailey); 158 (Paul Highnam); 173 (Paul Highnam); 175 (Jonathan Bailey).

Reproduced by permission of English Heritage (from the National Monuments Record at Swindon): 41 bottom right (FF86/411); 71 top (15076/18); 92 (3145/26); 155 (AA99/07779).

Reproduced by permission of English Heritage Special Events department: 6 (second from left, Neil Holmes); 27 (top row, centre; bottom row, right); 28 bottom; 42 bottom (Neil Holmes); 64 (Paul Lewis); 69 top (MLC); 70; 72 (Graeme Peacock); 80 (Neil Holmes); 82 (Paul Lewis); 83 (MLC); 91 (MLC); 93 (Neil Holmes); 97 (top row, centre; middle row, left; second from right; right); 107 top; 123 (Neil Holmes); 129 top (Nigel Corrie); 151 (middle row, right; bottom row, centre); 159 (Neil Holmes).

Reproduced by permission of the National Archives (formerly the Public Record Office, Kew): 18 top (PC2/58f.118); 30 top (SP14/216f.132), bottom (Pt.1/f. 90v SP14/216); 31 (RAIL 253/516); 37 bottom (LR2/124); 71 bottom (E31/2 243); 94 top (E31/2); 114 centre left (C115/91); 129 bottom (ASSI 44/54); 131 bottom (ADM 106/930 [90]); 147 bottom (MPH 1/ 387); 153 (RAIL 252/1); 154 top (HO45/79320); front and rear endpapers (from pages 131 and 114 respectively).

Item ... by ... ...
... mo ... Elizabeth
... primy ...
... of ...
... and purple ...
... out ...
... forrest of ...
... Exmple ...
... out ...
... on ...
... a very lytle ...
Item ... Ritsat ...
... of purple ...
blak ... ...

Item ... the xxxiij ...
... to ...
... of blanke ...
... of bla...